NEWSPAPERS...!

"Her style is clear, precise and full of in[...]
solved by parents."

"She promises over 100 parenting principles and the promise is abundantly fulfilled. Fun to read and bursting at the seams with good suggestions."   *-Boulder Daily Camera*

"... a tool box of information for those serious about parenting."
                                        -Santa Rosa Press Democrat

PROFESSIONALS...!

"A very unique and needed contribution in the area of dealing with children."   *-Ron Markovich, MSW, LSW II*

"The strength of this book is in its imaginative application of the principles to problem solving presented through a wide range of telling examples."   *-Individual Psychology Association of Washington D.C.*

PARENTS...!

"This book changed my life! My family is more peaceful now and there is a lot more cooperation."   *-Anne, Raleigh, North Carolina*

"Your book reads like a novel, which is surprising for a book so filled with helpful information."   *-Jim, St. Louis, Missouri*

"I was delighted with the change in my son's attitude. I found myself feeling affection and liking him. Something I had not experienced for some time."   *-Elaine, Denver, Colorado*

SUMMARY

Imagine a home where family members encourage each other, a home where they listen to each other and solve conflicts in a way that everyone wins! This book teaches you these skills and more! Led by a vision of empowered families, Kathryn Kvols has written an inspiring and motivating book that challenges parents, teachers, grandparents, coaches and others to create cooperative relationships with children. Drawing on her work counseling families and children, directing camps for children, and teaching personal and professional growth courses, Kvols examines the crucial issues that cause children to "misbehave." Based on Dr. Rudolf Dreikur's work, *Redirecting Children's Behavior*™ is a valuable resource for adults. You will learn to encourage children to have higher self-esteem and become responsible, cooperative citizens. It is a practical, step-by-step guide to redirecting behavior and reaching win/win situations. This book can also be used in conjunction with the 15-hour parenting course or the home course video.

OTHER PUBLICATIONS

Parenting Guidelines
Parenting Guidelines Audio Tape
Redirecting Children's Behavior Instructor Manual
Redirecting Children's Behavior Workbook
Redirecting For a Cooperative Classroom Instructor Manual
Redirecting For a Cooperative Classroom Workbook
Family Empowerment Series Instructor Manual
Family Empowerment Series Workbook
Understanding Yourself and Others
Redirecting Children's Behavior Home Course Video
Redirecting Children's Behavior Home Course Workbook

To our children's children.

ACKNOWLEDGMENTS

This work is the result of a life long passion for helping families. It has given my life great meaning to watch families become more empowering and cooperative. There are numerous people who have supported me that I would like to thank. I regret that I cannot list everyone.

First and foremost, I would like to thank my family; my husband, Brian, for his endless support, love and gentle nudgings; my son, Tyler, for being my teacher who taught me what unconditional love means; and Emily, Chloe, Amy and Cindy Harper who are teaching me what it means to become a blended family.

Thank you to my former husband, Bill Riedler who co-authored the first edition of this book. He also taught me how to teach and lead seminars. And I especially appreciate what a great father he is to our son.

Thank you to my staff; Betty Towry, Lois Hansler and Julia Szczes for their support and handling all the requests about, "When is the new book coming out!" Thanks to the instructors of the Redirecting Children's Behavior course. Their inspiration and dedication is making family life easier and more fun.

Helen Hall has been a wonderful source of inspiration and knowledge.

Thank you Bob Hoekstra and Julie Harrington for believing in me when I didn't.

Thank you to my editor, Tricia Bachus for being so incredibly meticulous, thorough and fun to work with.

The Global Relationship Centers have had a profound effect helping the International Network for Children and Families with our dream.

I acknowledge the late Rudolf Dreikurs, M.D. for being the source of inspiration for this work.

"Lord, make me an instrument of thy peace."
St. Francis of Assisi

Redirecting Children's Behavior

Table of Contents

FOREWORD

By Timothy J. Jordan, M.D.

I feel honored to write this introduction! I have experienced Kathryn Kvols as a friend, teacher, colleague, shoulder to cry on, teammate, consultant, visionary and spiritual director. The sense of inner peace and centeredness that she offers to everyone she touches is one of her greatest gifts. In a world yearning for a sense of peace and oneness, this book, and the work Kathryn is doing through the International Network for Children and Families, provides a template for action and growth for our society.

What we know and believe about children and families has changed dramatically in the last twenty-five years. Often parents, teachers and coaches recall the "good old days" when you could tell kids to do something and they jumped and did it! Kids today, on the other hand, are requesting respect and democracy, especially in the autocracies which control our homes, classrooms and athletic fields. This results in confusion and power struggles with parents and professionals and, often times, we are not even consciously aware of why we are struggling with our children!

If you step back and look at the progress we have made regarding understanding children, it is astonishing how far we have come in the last quarter of a century. It was not until the late 1960s and early 1970s, through the work of Dr. T. Berry Brazelton and others, that we became aware that infants could see and hear and feel and actively contribute to their relationships with their parents. How magnificent! With this finding, we began to view children, even at the beginning of their lives, as participants in the family process! Children have become more powerful, emphatic collaborators to be respected versus clay for us to mold and control. It is no wonder that many of us, as parents and professionals, have experienced confusion and chaos.

So here is Kathryn's book, *Redirecting Children's Behavior*, offering us the tools we need to develop the closeness with our children and families that we want so very much. Kathryn believes, as I do, that every person is born whole, complete, perfect and connected to everyone and everything. Through experiences as children, with parents, siblings, teachers and life as a whole, we are socialized and wounded in ways that cause us to lose our connections with others. Actually, we do not lose our connections, we just lose our awareness of them. This book, *Redirecting Children's Behavior*, takes us through the next step. It provides the framework and process for parenting so that we learn to relate with children in a way that supports their development; creating adults who feel whole and free and able to experience closeness and intimacy with others.

This book has been inspired by the *Redirecting Children's Behavior* course (offered through the International Network for Children and Families). In this course, parents, from all types of backgrounds with all kinds of children and concerns, are offered ways to make positive changes in their families. The process included in this book and in this class is not a "how to" format, but rather allows exploration of the ways we were parented, the decisions we made as children and how these experiences influence the way we parent. With this awareness, we are able to make more conscious, loving choices about how we want to parent and discipline our children. "RCB" teaches parents skills for empathetic listening, handling children's feelings, creating an encouraging atmosphere in our homes, decision-making, self-responsibility, win/win negotiation, using redirection to channel our children's mischievous energy in more positive ways and so much more! The end result is that children feel unconditionally loved, valued, empowered and safe. When children feel this way, much of their misbehavior disappears and is replaced by cooperation, closeness and fun. Your job as parent becomes one of gentle, but firm, guidance and support. I am excited that you care enough for your family, and yourself, to read this book and embark on a new path as a parent.

I want to encourage you a bit further. Participate in a parenting class. Do some personal growth work, through counseling, weekend retreats, seminars, reading or other avenues. Do couples work as we learn most about ourselves through our closest relationships. If you put yourself on such a journey of awareness, you will become more conscious of who you are, create more healthy relationships and parent children in a way that makes them feel loved, accepted and whole.

Parenting healthy, loving children is the most exciting and important result. Adults and children who feel loved and accepted have more love to give to others and, therefore, are more motivated to serve and give freely and joyously. And isn't this what life is all about? Thank you, Kathryn, for your love and commitment to all children and families and for your part in our "parenting evolution." This book expresses the essence of all you believe in and, for those of us who are parents, all that we hope for in our families.

Chapter 1

YOUR CHILD'S PERSPECTIVE

"I can't believe it!" said Justin's Mom. "It's as if Justin has a totally different attitude. Whenever he used to come home from playing in the park, he'd walk in crying and complaining about how the other kids were mistreating him. He was always getting into fights. He would never take any responsibility for anything and was continually blaming everybody else for his mistakes.

"Now when he comes home from the park, he enthusiastically tells me about how much fun he had with all his new friends. Justin's gotten into only one fight in the last three months! He even said to me, 'Mom, the other kids provoked me a lot, but I'm the one who actually broke the tent pole. It was my fault, so I'm going to buy the new pole.' He didn't blame anyone! It used to be a constant hassle when he was home, but now we really have fun together. I look forward to being with him."

Justin's Mom was reporting on the success she experienced after using the methods of Rudolf Dreikurs, M. D. that form the basis for this book. These methods are incorporated into parenting principles that you can use to redirect children's behavior. It is possible to put these methods into practice simply from reading this book. Using this book as a companion to the *Redirecting Children's Behavior*™ parenting classes or the *Redirecting Children's Behavior* home course will increase your learning as you get the opportunity to role-play with your classmates and hear their stories of success. These classes are offered through the International Network for Children and Families. Later in this book, you will read the details of Justin's story and how his behavior was redirected. Then you'll more fully understand his Mom's enthusiastic response to the changes in her son.

What is redirecting?

Redirecting is a form of discipline that is firm and kind with the goal in mind that the child assumes responsibility for his or her actions. The purpose is to encourage the child to become intrinsically (or inner) motivated rather than motivated by external circumstances or events. The redirecting principle defines discipline as guidance and teaching with an emphasis on mutual respect. This method teaches natural and logical consequences for a child's inappropriate behavior instead of punishment and results in enhancing your child's self-esteem and cooperation skills.

Redirecting is not about giving you new "techniques" that you can use "on" your child to make him stop misbehaving. These methods are not about controlling or manipulating your child. Redirecting is a way of life that focuses on creating win/win situations in which no one is the loser, not the parent, the teacher, the coach, nor the child. When children sense that you are not trying to control them but that you are trying to make you both winners, then they are more respectful and cooperative.

Why not use punishment?

Punishment breeds fear. While it may result in the child immediately stopping the behavior, it is providing only an illusion that it is effective. If you carefully observe a child after he has been punished, you will see him finding ways to get even with the punisher like, picking on younger siblings or pets, getting bad grades at school, destroying his property or yours, running away from home, and "forgetting" to do chores. The list of negative reactions can go on and on.

With punishment, the locus or locality of control for the behavior becomes external, not internal. The child is dependent on the authority figure who must be present and elicit fear in the child. Punishment is not effective in developing self-responsibility. Instead, with punishment as the form of discipline, children often try to "get away with" the misbehavior, rather than develop their own moral standards. When you use punishment, the child either becomes compliant or resistant and revengeful. After being punished, a child often focuses on "getting even" with the authority figure rather than thinking about the consequences of his inappropriate behavior and what he learned from his behavior.

The opposite of behavior being controlled by an authority figure is an internal locus of control maintained by the child's set of internalized values. The child learns self-responsibility and behaves in ways that he feels are "right" for him.

Punishment also carries some side effects such as low self esteem, acting or responding out of fear, a confusion about being hurt by someone who is supposed to love you, and support for the belief that over-powering someone is the way to get what you want. In addition, it creates a lack of trust and teaches children to hide their mistakes.

Check in with yourself the next time you punish your child. Are you acting out of anger, hurt, wanting to hurt back, or feeling your sense of powerlessness? Next time, stop, get quiet, and reevaluate your response. Ask yourself, "What is it I really want to teach my child right now?"

What about using rewards?

Another traditional approach to discipline that creates dependency on an authority figure or external locus of control is the practice of rewarding. Rewards used to bait or bribe children to get a desired behavior invariably backfire. Children begin to focus on how to get more and better rewards rather than on the feelings of doing their best or doing something helpful for someone else. We often feel the most valuable when we do something for someone else and expect nothing in return. Rewards will interfere with the development of feeling worthwhile. Children may also interpret being rewarded as a message that they don't need to do anything unless there is something in it for them. External rewards prev͏e ͭhe child from relying on an internal sense of self-confiden satisfaction.

What should the goal of discipline be?

The goal of discipline should be to teach alternate behaviors to replace inappropriate ones. It must also teach a child to be self-responsible and to respond in appropriate ways that get positive results, whether the authority figure is present or not. Discipline should also increase a child's awareness of her choices and it is the choices she makes that make her happy or unhappy. By doing this, the locus of control becomes internal and contributes to the child's self-esteem. Discipline should also build self-esteem. Children misbehave when they feel discouraged or powerless and when you use discipline methods that overpower them or make them feel bad about themselves, you lower their self-esteem. It doesn't make sense to punish a child who is already feeling badly about herself and heap more discouragement on top of her.

There is so much more you can do to make parenting more enjoyable and help your children develop attitudes that will prepare them for the challenges of adulthood. As you begin this important process, keep in mind that many of the principles suggested may take some time and persistence before you can enjoy the results.

For instance, if you had the task of pressing eighty-eight levers at prescribed intervals at a certain speed and, at any given time, you would have to switch to a different set of levers using a different speed, could you do it? What I just described was someone playing a piano. All of us know that to play the piano takes practice. The same is true with these parenting principles. They take practice. At first you may feel uncomfortable or you find they may not work the way you were expecting. With patience and practice you will become a more confident parent. Remember to be gentle with yourself when you make mistakes.

Another component to your success in learning a new way of parenting is to have trust in your child's ability to learn. This is especially difficult since we have been trained to underestimate our children and that notion may cause us to give up too early and miss the joy and freedom of having responsible children. So, follow through, trust, and allow yourself mistakes, and you'll be amazed at what you and your child can accomplish.

ASK YOURSELF, "HOW DOES MY CHILD SEE IT?"

Whether we know it or not, we are constantly influencing the way in which our children develop their attitudes about life. If we want to become more effective in assisting our children to develop in responsible, cooperative ways, we must begin with a clear understanding of three factors:

1. How does my child interpret the meaning of his experiences?

2. Which experiences are most likely to influence the development of my child's attitudes?

3. In what way do I have the ability to change those experiences or modify my child's interpretations?

Before implementing a specific discipline method, explore the answers to these three questions so you not only know what to do, but why it works.

Children come into this world with a tremendous disadvantage. Not only are they considerably smaller than and dependent upon adults, but their contributions go unnoticed by our society. In order to better understand what influences your child, you must look at situations from her point of view. By looking at situations from this perspective, parents can often avoid doing the things that make their child feel powerless and contribute to an inaccurate self-concept of himself. Instead, you can find ways to restructure situations to help your child discover his own strengths and abilities.

For instance, when a toddler cries for a toy, we might respond by doing either more than required or less than necessary. On some occasions, we may be doing less by ignoring the child's crying, making him feel more helpless. On other occasions, we may do more than required by bringing the toy to the child so that he doesn't have to reach for the toy.

Why is that doing too much? Because if our goal as a parent is to create self-reliance, then we'd want to position the toy so that our toddler would be encouraged to reach for the toy and discover for himself what it takes to get it.

Gentle coaxing and observing what he can and cannot do leads to gradually increasing the amount of effort the toddler can contribute toward his own satisfaction. These early lessons in self-reliance will be far more successful than doing everything for your child up until he's eighteen-years-old and then saying, "You're an adult now, take care of yourself!" By starting early, we can avoid having to compensate for the dependency we've created through years of overprotection and doing too much for the child.

Our task as parents is to take helpless, dependent children and guide their experiences and assist them in realizing that they can become self-confident and cooperative individuals.

We must be sensitive to the fact that our success in achieving this goal does not depend upon our good intentions, but upon our child's interpretations. These interpretations are the final modifiers of every interaction with our child. With each redirecting method you use, ask yourself, "How does my child see it?"

WHAT MAKES CHILDREN THE WAY THEY ARE?

We all have biases and it is important that we do. Without being prejudiced, we wouldn't have the ability to take action because we would be so intimidated by what might occur in the next moment of life. Our personality is our unique, personal collection of biases and expectations about life which we use to help us choose our actions.

For example, if we feel it is safe or advantageous to walk through an unknown doorway, we will do it without hesitation. But if we feel it is unsafe, we will hesitate or refuse to go. The decision, however, is ultimately based on our expectations and not on reality.

It isn't surprising that we formed most of these expectations or generalized prejudices in childhood. We learned to "size up" our predicaments and create a lifestyle which we used to deal with life. So, starting at a very young age, children begin formulating these concepts in order to know:

> -What to expect from life.
> -What to expect from men.
> -What to expect from women.

-What to expect from their own abilities.
-What their best method for handling any situation is.

MAJOR INFLUENCES

These beliefs, which are based upon our child's interpretation of early experiences, are often taken into adulthood and become the source of many adult conflicts. The reason for this is that these beliefs are formed when our child is in a position of disadvantage as explained earlier and there is a tremendous chance for misinterpretation. Some of the major influences that the child may misinterpret are:

Birth Order
Age Differences
Sex
Handicaps (or Health Problems)
Social Settings
Tragedies in the Family
Sibling Competition
Family Values
Parental Responses

Birth order

Whether a child is the first, the only, the middle, or the "baby" will dramatically structure how he finds his place in the world. His birth order position can modify or shape his conclusions about life and finding significance which will, in turn, influence his personality.

The oldest child at first sees a world in which he is the main event in the lives of the adults. He then loses his "specialness" with the arrival of the second child. He may experience this as being dethroned.

The second child must, from the start, establish her place, not only with the adults, but also with her sibling. Each subsequent child will be presented a different situation in which to discover his place in the family.

John was an only child for three years. At first, he found his place by equating attention with love. But when his sister arrived, part of Mother's attention understandably shifted to the new infant. Although it was not reality, John felt dethroned and unloved so he started hitting the baby. This always resulted in gaining Mother's immediate, but negative, attention and negative attention was better to John than being ignored.

Because of his birth order and other contributing factors, John was learning to be important by misbehaving. Meanwhile, his sister was being introduced to a totally different view of the world. Without apparent cause, she was being attacked. This situation might lead her to conclude that the world is a scary place. Even Mother's soothing responses might encourage her to feel, "I can be special by complaining about someone picking on me." It is possible that birth order might play a part in her eventual choice of a husband. She may be inclined to choose a mate who victimizes her in some way.

Of course, not every second child interprets her experiences as "the world is scary." Many other influencing factors play a part. Each child sees these situations in her own way. Another child might interpret the identical situation as "I must fight unfairness." Instead of becoming a victim, she might become a lawyer and make a career of fighting unfairness.

Age differences

The amount of time between the births of children will also influence their interactions. An eighteen-month-old who has a baby sister might struggle to remain "more capable." However, a four-year-old who has a baby sister may develop the role of the "super responsible" child by being helpful to mom with the baby.

In a family with an eight-, seven- and two-year-old, you might find that the eight- and seven-year-old will form an alliance and become additional parents for the two-year-old. In this case, it would be very easy for the baby to become the charmer who gets others to do things for him.

So, be aware of how each of your children is fitting into the family. Their behavior will give you clues as to how they are perceiving their significance in the family.

Sex

As the result of our traditional role models, we often have different expectations for boys than we do for girls. In the past, we used to encourage aggression and stoicism in boys and we encouraged dependence and passivity in girls. These roles are changing, but we still have few role models of "equality" between the sexes. Our expectations of these roles and even our confusion about them have a profound influence on our children's perceptions.

In the Johnson family, there is an eight-year-old boy, and a six-year-old girl. When the boy gets hurt and starts to cry, the parents respond by saying, "Stop crying and be a big boy!" Whereas when the girl gets hurt and cries, she is comforted and her tears are accepted.

In this situation, the son is being taught to hide his feelings and to influence people with his strength. The girl is being taught to influence people by using helplessness and dependence. What most children lack is a role model who balances strength, vulnerability, and open, honest expression of feelings. Perhaps a way to encourage that with our children would be to take the same example above and change our responses as the parent. Whether it is our son or our daughter who gets hurt and cries, we could acknowledge their hurt, allow them to cry, and encourage them both to find ways that they could make themselves feel better. Eliminating the stereotypical phrases that we automatically say to our sons or daughters is also a good first step to creating those new role models.

Handicaps or health problems

A child with a handicap or health problem does have a disadvantage. However, he also has a choice: "Do I want to feel sorry for myself or do I want to develop strengths to overcome my disability?" One determining factor will be the amount of courage the child has.

Ten-year-old Leslie had asthma and when Mother asked her to do her share of the house work, she frequently had an attack. This made Mother suspicious and when she explored this situation further, she looked at Leslie's place in the family as the second child of four. Through talking to Leslie I found that she was feeling, "My sister is special because she's the oldest. Mike is the only boy and Amy's the baby in the family. Everyone's special, except me!"

Looking at her position from Leslie's point of view, it might be concluded that Leslie was exploiting her health problem because she felt discouraged. She didn't feel special or that she had a place in the family. When her Mother recognized that Leslie was using her asthma attacks to get noticed and to feel special, she started using methods to redirect Leslie's inappropriate behavior. She responded to Leslie's attacks differently and she provided many opportunities for Leslie to feel special, such as allowing her to occasionally plan and cook a meal by herself. As a result of Mother's efforts to redirect Leslie, her asthma attacks decreased dramatically.

In this situation, Leslie's asthma was real. However, until Leslie's Mother understood what was happening from Leslie's point of view and changed her response to the attacks, Leslie was getting the payoff of special attention through having attacks. When it became a disadvantage for her to have asthma attacks, then Leslie had fewer attacks.

Many people like Stevie Wonder and Ray Charles, owe their success and fame to the extra energy they have put toward overcoming a physical handicap. At some point, they were faced with the choice of submitting to the handicap and drawing others into their service or compensating for the handicap by developing exceptional talents and abilities. The courage to look at these choices will determine the effect that a physical or emotional handicap will have on a child. And parents can facilitate a healthy choice by being sensitive to what a child is perceiving and changing any of their responses that contribute to their child's ineffective choices.

Social setting

Today's children are being brought up in a rapidly changing society. They are being confronted with moral decisions at a much earlier age than most of us were. Along with these changes, demands for equal rights are becoming more frequent as women, homosexuals, racial minorities, and the handicapped struggle for recognition as "equals." Our children are involved in this struggle as well. This is evident by comments like, "You can't boss me around," that are communicated (verbally and nonverbally) at home and at school. This presents a problem for parents and teachers who were brought up in authoritarian families.

A conflict occurs when we try to use traditional parenting methods with children who feel equal. When these traditional methods fail, we tend to question our ability to be effective parents and we fail to recognize that we are social pioneers. It is important that we realize that we are having difficulties with our marriages and our children because we are exploring new roles and not because we are inept. Our challenge is to develop new ways to live together as equals even though we have few examples to use as models. So, be easy on yourself when you find your old ways aren't effective and the new ways are still cumbersome.

Tragedies in the family

Losses, such as a terminal illness, a death in the family, a separation, or a divorce can frequently evoke a temporary feeling of insecurity for a child. However, parents or caregivers need to be careful to avoid feeling sorry for a child experiencing one of those losses.

When we excuse behavior because of a loss ("He's from a 'broken home,' so don't be too hard on him."), we are training that child to feel entitled to do whatever he wants because life is difficult for him. This does not prepare him to deal with the unfairness that is an inevitable part of living. We all must experience losses. It's not as important that the child has experienced a loss as it is that we help him deal with the loss in appropriate ways. Our responses to tragedies will also influence our child.

Mother was pregnant with her second child and she asked three-year-old Maggie to bring her sewing basket down from upstairs. Maggie went up the stairs happy to be helping her Mother. As she descended the stairs, with sewing basket in hand, Maggie tripped on her shoelaces and fell down the stairs and was killed. Four months later Mom had her second child.

Mother's response to this tragedy will definitely influence the attitudes of her second child. There are any number of possible responses that this mother might have towards this child. She might overprotect and make few demands on her which might create the child's feeling that no one has a right to make demands on her. Or, the child might learn that she can get Mother's undivided attention by being careless or accident-prone. Also, if Mother idealizes the child who was killed, it will be impossible for this second child to live up to the first child being a "saint."

If there has been a tragedy in your family, look to see how your child is behaving. If your child's behavior is inappropriate, check to see if you are responding to her in a way that might be perpetuating the problem.

Sibling competition

Sibling competition does not necessarily mean outward aggression shown by one sibling against the other. Competition, as Dreikurs defined it, is the process whereby one child gives up in an area where his sibling succeeds. He does this in order to avoid comparison. One child might excel in music and the other sibling might excel in sports. Often the child who doesn't do well in the area of his sibling's expertise feels that he does not have talent in that area. In reality, he has only given up. With practice, he too could achieve in that area, if he chooses. Here is an example of sibling competition:

Bill is a friend of mine who plays the drums and has excellent rhythm. I noticed, though, that he didn't like dancing. I was confused that someone with such good rhythm would be hesitant to be on a dance floor. One day we were looking through his family album and I saw a picture of his older sister in a gorgeous fur-lined dance costume. Bill explained that she was an excellent dancer and got special attention from their family for her talent. I shared with Bill the possibility that he may have given up in that area. He actually felt that he was not a good dancer. After our discussion, Bill recognized that it's not that he's a clumsy dancer, but that he had given up practicing as a result of the competition he felt with his sister. When he realized that, he decided he was going to enjoy dancing more.

Having one "good" child and one "bad" child is a characteristic of sibling competition. The "bad" child feels that there is no way he can be as good as his sibling. But he does get noticed by being the "bad" child and the "good" child often feels he's only important if he can be better than his misbehaving sibling. The "good" child may even try to get the "bad" child into trouble by tattling on him, or provoking him to misbehave in order to maintain their roles.

In one of our RCB classes, a parent said, "I can't believe that my good child would actually provoke her brother. She's always so cooperative." One of the other mothers got a sheepish grin on her face and proceeded to tell this story.

"I have to confess, in my family, I was the "good" girl and I had a brother who was always getting punished. One time we were in back of the garage where there was a sledge hammer and I looked at him and said, 'Boy, that sure looks heavy doesn't it?' He said, 'Yeah, it sure does.' Tauntingly I said, 'I bet it would really hurt if someone got hit with it.' He got a big grin on his face, and began to pick it up. I said, 'If you hit me with that, I'm telling!' He picked it up and tapped me on the shoulder with it. I ran into the house screaming, 'Mommy, Andy hit me with a sledge hammer!' Mother held and rocked me until I quieted down and then she lectured and spanked Andy and I felt pretty smug about the whole thing."

So, you can see that sometimes the younger sibling is not the poor innocent victim that we think. If you have a "good" child and a "bad" child, and you decide to change that, be prepared for some surprises. When you start being effective with the "bad" child, he will start being more responsible. It is possible that your "good" child may start to misbehave. At this point, believe it or not, this is a sign of progress. The "good" child is having difficulty being better than the "bad" child, who has started to become more responsible. This forces the "good" child to start shopping for other ways to be special. If the "good" child starts misbehaving, pat yourself on the back because it means that you have succeeded in making the misbehavior of both children inappropriate. You have disturbed the equilibrium.

If you have provided opportunities during this change for both children to find a place through teamwork and helpfulness, this switch to misbehavior won't occur. But even if it does, the new misbehavior is easy to redirect by emphasizing teamwork between the two. Give them jobs they can do together like grocery shopping, or encourage them to play cooperative games (See Suggested Reading). "Putting them in the same boat," (Chapter 4) will also expedite cooperation.

Here is an example that depicts the disturbance of equilibrium.

> I was counseling a seventeen-year-old named John who was coming home drunk a lot. He would get sick all over the furniture and new white carpeting which created a lot of chaos with his family. He was also failing school and did not have many friends. In contrast, his fifteen-year-old brother, Kevin, earned excellent grades, had many friends, and was the "model" child, keeping his room neat and organized.

> I worked with John for several months and he finally began making significant progress. He quit coming home drunk, got a job and started making acceptable grades. The biggest change, however, was that when he got home from school, he would begin working on projects instead of absorbing himself in television.

> Six months after I had terminated with John, I got a call from his parents saying that Kevin had begun failing school and been caught stealing. This behavior was easy to redirect because the parents intervened early before the pattern had developed over a long period of time.

Family values

All the children in a family frequently adopt values that are shared by both mother and father. For example, both mother and father might value education. As a result, all the children might attend college. The exception to this is the "black sheep," who, to gain significance, adopts the opposite value.

Parental response

This is the most important influence because it is within our control. As adults we can consciously decide how we will respond. The way we respond gives us the opportunity to change children's experiences or to modify their interpretation of those experiences.

Very often children base their future behavior on how the parents respond to their behavior initially. If their behavior elicits a rewarding response, they will try that behavior again. When using the term "rewarding," it does not necessarily mean rewarding in a positive way. The child may find it rewarding to challenge parents and watch them become upset.

Here are three ways a parent may respond to a child who has just scratched her leg. Remember, your child is looking at your reactions to know how to behave.

Beth has been playing happily outside. Suddenly she runs in the house, sobbing slightly, and approaches Mother who is peeling potatoes at the kitchen sink. She tugs on Mother's shirt and says, "Mommy, Mommy, I scratched my leg." Mother puts down the potatoes, scoops up Beth and puts her on the counter in front of her. "Oh, you poor dear!" Mother says with a very worried look on her face as she examines the scratch that is red but not bleeding. "Do you want me to kiss it and make it better?" Beth has begun to cry harder and twists her leg in pain as her Mother examines it. She nods her head, unable to speak because she is crying so loudly. Mother hugs her closely and says, "Let Mommy carry you in and wash it off so we can put a bandage on it."

Notice how much attention Beth is getting for her scratch. Mother is being too kind and if Mother continues this type of response, Beth may learn that she can get special attention when she is hurt. She may grow up to become "accident prone" or learn to become dependent on others to take care of her and make her feel better.

However, sometimes parents are too firm rather than too kind.

Beth has been playing happily outside. Suddenly she runs in the house, sobbing slightly, and approaches Mother who is peeling potatoes at the kitchen sink. She tugs on Mother's sleeve and says, "Mommy, Mommy, I scratched my leg." Mother continues peeling potatoes and acts annoyed at the interruption. In a disgusted tone of voice, she snaps, "That's only a scratch. You aren't going to die."

In the above example, Mother's response may have been interpreted by Beth as, "No one cares about how I feel." Mother also denied Beth's right to feel. Beth may learn to "stuff" her feelings. Mother was definitely being too firm. In this case, Beth learns that she needs to be independent because no one will be there for her when she needs support.

Here is the approach I would suggest:

Beth has been playing happily outside. Suddenly she runs in the house, sobbing slightly, and approaches Mother who is peeling potatoes at the kitchen sink. She tugs on Mother's shirt and says, "Mommy, Mommy, I scratched my leg." Mother bends down to Beth's size, looks at the scratch and begins to rub Beth's back lightly. She empathizes, "That looks like it might hurt." Beth feels the comfort of being understood and accepted and nods her head. "What do you think you could do to make yourself feel better?" Mother asks. Beth shrugs her shoulders but her crying has diminished, "I don't know." Mother smiles at Beth and asks, "Well, what have you seen me do when I cut myself?" Beth's face brightens and she says, "Put a bandage on?" Mother nods her head in agreement and suggests, "Yes, and you may want to wash it to get rid of the germs. Do you want some help?"

In this example, Mother's response is communicating the idea, "Life is full of bumps and scrapes. It's important that you learn to pick yourself up, brush yourself off and put on your own bandages." Here the child is learning that she is responsible for how she feels and for taking care of herself. And, Mother is there to offer support. Mother was being kind and firm at the same time. Her child learns interdependence, that she can handle life's problems and that if she needs support, she can get it.

It is difficult to avoid our first inclination, which is to do whatever we can to make the child feel better. However, if we do not resist this temptation, we may teach the child to be dependent on someone else to relieve her pain.

We often underestimate the tremendous influence our responses have on our children. Below is an example of a child who got attention for negative behavior because she didn't succeed in getting attention in a positive way.

One mother told me how she had seen her twenty-month-old daughter get her father's attention using a very creative technique.

Her daughter was sitting quietly rocking in her rocking chair as her father read his newspaper. She began to rock faster and faster until the rocking chair tipped over, spilling her to the floor with the chair on top of her. Immediately, the father dropped his newspaper, ran over, picked up the chair and rescued his daughter. He carried her in his arms to his chair and spent fifteen minutes comforting her in his lap.

About three days later, the girl approached her father who again was reading the newspaper. She tried climbing onto his lap but Dad was being uncooperative. Dad gently brushed her aside saying, "Not now, honey, I want to read the paper." As Mother watched unobserved, the little girl walked over to the rocking chair, looked back at her father who was absorbed in the daily news, tipped the chair forward until its back rested on the floor. Quietly she squirmed under the tipped over chair and started crying. Success! Dad threw down his newspaper, rushed to pick her up, and consoled her in his lap again.

Negative attention is better than no attention and often our children prefer negative attention to being ignored. In the above example, the little girl was willing to settle for her father's concern for her in an inappropriate way when she was unable to get his positive attention.

RECOMMENDATION:

Draw a picture of your family, depicting what each person does to feel that he has a special place.

Chapter 2

REDIRECTING BEHAVIOR

WHAT'S WRONG WITH THIS PICTURE?

Three people came into the doctor's office with three different problems.

Doctor: "What seems to be your problem?"
Patient A: "I have a headache."
Patient B: "My foot hurts a lot."
Patient C: "My arm hurts whenever it's cold outside."
Doctor: "I can help you all! Since none of you feels good, I'll take out your gall bladders. That will help. Why, just six months ago, I had a patient who didn't feel good and I took out his gall bladder and now he feels fine!"

If you didn't feel well, would you go to this doctor? Of course not, because he didn't take the time to make the proper *diagnosis* before suggesting action. A doctor who assumes that all of our problems are the same and that one technique can be the remedy for any discomfort does not promote our confidence in his medical skills.

The necessity for taking the time to make a correct diagnosis is obvious in the medical field; however, we sometimes overlook its importance in the field of parenting.

Sometimes when I lecture, I will open my talk the way the doctor began with his three patients; by asking them to identify their individual complaints about their children's behavior.

> "My son talks back and won't obey."
> "My daughter sucks her thumb."
> "They're fighting all the time."
> "Wets the bed."
> "She's lazy and always forgets."

In this book and in the RCB course, you will find discussions and explanations of many methods parents can use to redirect children's behavior. But, as soon as I start discussing one method, parents will often ask, "Will that solve the bed wetting?" "What about using that with thumb sucking?"

Unfortunately, no one method will be effective in every situation. In order to determine which methods to use, you must first take the time to identify or diagnose your child's purpose for misbehaving. Until you understand the unique goal for your child's misbehavior, your choice of action may prove to be ineffective.

WHY CHILDREN MISBEHAVE

> "I give them a lot of attention and I show my children that I love them, so why do they still misbehave?"

It is unfortunate in our society that we discriminate against two age groups, children and the elderly, in regard to their ability to contribute. One of the reasons why people misbehave, in general, is because they don't feel worthwhile or they feel their contributions are not valuable.

A mother came to me concerned about her daughter's misbehavior. She had begun making frequent statements like, "I'm going to run away!" or "I want to kill myself." When I asked the daughter why she felt that way, her simple answer was, "Because I'm not important at home."

In the past, children were needed, particularly in fa communities where they made valuable contributions. Becau᠍ major changes in our lifestyles, it has become more difficult for children to find a place in which to contribute and feel needed. Our society still hasn't responded to the challenge of providing new ways for children to feel valuable.

Even adults want to feel that they belong or have value. When we have a feeling of belonging, we are willing to participate, to cooperate and enjoy life fully. We are also able to look at the demands of a situation to determine what would be helpful to ourselves and the group. In essence, belonging is feeling valuable.

So, when we feel discouraged or don't belong, we have a tendency to misbehave. Perhaps we misbehave by feeling sorry for ourselves, feeling the need to prove ourselves, or by giving up. We usually misbehave for the purpose of getting others to respond in some way. Children misbehave because they doubt their ability to find a place of belonging through contribution and cooperation. They feel unable to live up to an adult's high standards so they discover that they easily achieve significance through misbehavior. Then our love for them causes us to become overly-concerned with their misbehavior. This is a mistaken and unsatisfying way to find a place of belonging because it doesn't result in feeling worthwhile.

The bottom line is: Loving your children is not enough. Provide opportunities for them to feel worthwhile and useful through their contributions. You will learn how to help the child feel valuable under the section of "Redirecting Power" later in this chapter.

RECOGNIZING THE CHILD'S GOALS

Rudolf Dreikurs referred to the misbehaving child's purpose as a mistaken goal. He classified misbehavior into four general goals: attention, power, revenge and avoidance. Use these four goals as the starting point for identifying your children's mistaken goals. I am not suggesting that you attempt to pigeonhole all children to fit neatly into one of these four goals because each child is a unique individual. The goals can be used, however, to guide you toward an understanding of a child's purpose. **Misbehavior is communication.** When we see misbehavior as bad, then we want to control our children which often results in use of intimidation tactics. When we see misbehavior as communication, we ask ourselves, "What is my child trying to communicate to me?" This allows us to feel less threatened and more able to redirect the behavior.

*****

The Goal Of Attention

Mother and her best friend have gotten together for a visit. They are sitting on the sofa in the living room. Four-year-old Billy runs into the room and stands behind the sofa. In a whiny voice, he asks, "Mom, where's my airplane?" Mom stops talking to her friend and says, "I'm busy now. It's in your room." She resumes talking to her friend. Billy interrupts again, "Where in my room?" This time Mom interrupts her friend and says, "In your toy chest...I'm sorry, what were you saying?" Mom turns her attention back on her friend. Billy persists, "Would you help me find it?" Mother looks at him angrily and snaps, "Not right now! Can't you see I'm busy?" Billy begins to whine louder, "But Mommy!" Mother jumps from the sofa in exasperation, "Oh all right! But when I find it, I want you to play with it in your room so I can visit with my friend."

This sounds like an innocent request for help, right? However, what would be a more acceptable way for the child to respond to this situation? Wouldn't it be more appropriate for the child to recognize that Mother is involved with her friend, make his request once, and then respect Mother's request by either finding the toy himself, or by getting interested in something else? What is the purpose for his behavior? What does he want from his mother? It's as if the child is equating being the center of the adult's attention with being loved.

In this example, the child's inappropriate demands for attention were made in a relatively positive way. When a child is more discouraged, his demands for attention may be more negative. For example, the child might start playing with something he's not allowed to play with, throw a temper tantrum, or pick a fight with his brother or sister. Some other forms of attention-getting are whining, dawdling, forgetting, acting helpless, interrupting, or repeating an annoying behavior.

Dreikurs suggested that the way you can identify the mistaken goal is by the way you feel and by how you would usually respond. For the child whose mistaken goal is attention, the adult tends to feel frustrated and annoyed. She would normally tend to respond by giving negative attention. Not all children, though, use negative behavior to get attention. Consider the child who is being good to get attention. It is important for her to be "good" and to please. This child is often referred to as the "goodie-goodie" at home and at school. Again, your response is important. When you feel annoyed by this child's continual striving to please you or be "good," it is an indication her misdirected goal is attention.

Redirecting The Goal Of Attention

There are four steps to redirecting the goal of attention.

1. Make no eye contact with the child who is acting inappropriately.
2. Do not talk to the child. So far, I have described ignoring the child when he is trying to get your attention, but ignoring is not enough. If you just ignore, the behavior is likely to escalate.
3. Do something to make the child feel loved. The best way to do this is to rub her back or stroke her hair. Don't pat your child's head because that is demeaning.
4. Take action immediately, do the first three steps, no eye contact, no words and do something to make the child feel loved as soon as you start feeling annoyed. Do not wait. If you wait, you will start getting angry and then it will be difficult not to react angrily. Or it might be more difficult to do something to make the child feel loved.

When you practice doing all four steps correctly, your child has to do some rethinking. She is used to feeling, "As long as I keep an adult busy with me, then I am loved." Now she sees that she is loved without the adult having to "keep busy" with her.

A father in the parenting course had learned about the misdirected goal of attention and decided he wanted to respond to his daughter's attempt at attention in a different way. One day, he was talking across the fence in his backyard to his neighbor. His daughter had a habit of interrupting him while he was talking. His goal was for her to wait patiently until he finished and then politely say, "Excuse me" like he had previously taught her to do. However, she had other plans. She began whining immediately, "Dadddddy!" He kept on talking with his neighbor, did not talk to her or make eye contact with her. He lovingly started rubbing her back as she stood whining beside him. She continued to whine for a few seconds and stopped. Then she patiently waited for a break in their conversation and said, "Excuse me, Daddy," very politely.

At the parenting course the next week, he couldn't wait to tell of his success. He was honest enough to tell us he had been very skeptical of the steps for redirecting when they had been presented initially. But now he was a firm believer in their effectiveness.

In order for successful redirection to occur, it is vital that you take time to be with your child when she is not vying for attention. This helps to reinforce the appropriate behavior you desire.

Another method you can use with a young child, is to remove your child from the situation. If you choose this method, there are a few things you can do to make it work easier for you. First of all, pick your child up in a loving way and put her in a room (preferably not her own bedroom so she doesn't see her room as a place of punishment), and say once, and only once, "You can come back when you are ready." This gives her an internal locus of control. If you say, "Come out in five minutes," it has become an external locus of control. This concept is discussed under "Self-quieting" in Chapter Seven. If your child comes out right away and acts appropriately, great! If she comes back and continues to act inappropriately, immediately and lovingly pick her up again and take her out of the room, but this time don't say a thing! You may have to take her out of the room several times. Be patient and persistent.

When my son Tyler was two-and-a-half, I had invited some friends over for dinner. At dinner, Tyler started acting inappropriately and I first asked him to stop. He calmed down for a few seconds and then began to misbehave again. I gently picked him up and brought him to another room and said, "You may come back when you are ready." He came back immediately and continued to act inappropriately. I picked him up and took him out of the room and this time I didn't say a thing. He came in again and acted inappropriately. This time his father took him out. We must have taken him out of the room fourteen times. After the fourteenth time, Tyler sat for a whole hour at the table without being inappropriate.

One thing that is nice about couples using the same principles is that you can alternate so that one parent does not get overly frustrated. You may be thinking, "Fourteen times! Who has the time to do that?!" Yes, it took patience to do this the first time but the more I used the method, the more quickly Tyler's behavior became appropriate.

Teach your child how to get your attention in appropriate ways. One mother taught her daughter to say, "I need some attention, Mommy," instead of acting out to get it. When her daughter said those words, Mom would either give her the attention right then or she would negotiate a specific, agreed upon time with her child.

A busy parent can make "dates" with her children and each child can get a separate date during the week. The dates may consist of a breakfast, meeting the child at school for lunch, roller skating, fishing, etc. These one-on-one times are essential. It is much easier for a child to share intimate thoughts and feelings when he is alone with you in a non-hurried atmosphere. Times like these build your relationship with your child and if he feels he has a close relationship with you, he becomes more respectful and more cooperative with you. When children can get our attention in appropriate ways, they are less likely to get it in inappropriate ways.

You might be thinking that these steps wouldn't work for your child and you may be right, especially if your child has a different goal than attention. So read on!

*****

The Goal Of Power

"Turn the TV off," Dad said to Michael. "It's time for bed." "Aw, Dad, let me finish watching this one show. It'll be over in thirty minutes," challenges Michael. "No, I said turn it off!" Dad demands with a stern look on his face. "Why? I'll just watch fifteen minutes, OK? C'mon, let me watch it - you never let me stay up late anymore," Michael protests. Dad's face is getting red and he points his finger at Michael, "Did you hear what I said, young man? I said off with the TV. . . NOW!"

Michael and Dad are in a power struggle. When a child attempts to use his power, it is usually the result of earlier attempts at getting attention being met by an overpowering adult's reactions. The child interprets the parent's use of power as, "You get people to do what you want when you have the power," or, "Overpowering others is a viable solution." It is as if the child responds to authority by saying, "You can't make me." Often the child is willing to sustain the pain of punishment in order to gain the satisfaction of feeling powerful by defeating the authority figure. If we spank the child, it is likely that we will only encourage him to use force in his future attempts to influence others.

The adult in this type of situation usually feels angry at being challenged. The natural inclination is to try to use more power. A clue to helping you differentiate between power and attention-getting behavior is what your child does. When you discipline your child who is seeking attention, his misbehavior stops because he has achieved his goal. He has your attention. However, when you discipline a child with the goal of power, his misbehavior usually escalates rather than stops. Even if the behavior stops temporarily, you can distinguish it from the goal of attention by watching the expression on his child's face. He will have a defiant look as if he were saying, "You may be able to stop me now, but I'll defeat you later!"

Redirecting The Goal Of Power

1. Ask yourself, "How can I give my child more power in this situation?"

When you find yourself in power struggles with your children, change the question from, "What can I do to control this situation?" to "How can I give my child more power in this situation?"

One time when Tyler was three years old, he and I went grocery shopping around 5:30 p.m. This was a mistake because I was tired and he was tired and I was trying to hurry to get home to prepare supper. I put him in the shopping cart to expedite the shopping. As I hurried down each aisle picking out my purchases, Tyler began throwing out the groceries I had put in. At first I said in a calm manner, "Tyler, please stop." He ignored me and continued throwing things out of the cart. Then I said more harshly, "Tyler, STOP IT!" As my voice rose, along with my anger, his behavior escalated. Next he took my purse and dumped the contents all over the store floor. I grabbed his small arms as he picked up a can of tomatoes to throw on top of my purse contents. At that instant I understood how child abuse occurs, because I wanted to shake him. Fortunately I realized what was happening.

I took a few steps back and counted to ten, which is a method I use when I calm myself. As I was counting, I realized that Tyler had no power in that situation. He was tired and had been forced into a cold, hard shopping cart seat as his harried mother rushed through the store picking up items he didn't even care about. So, instead of asking myself, "How can I get this situation under control?," I asked myself, "What can I do to make Tyler feel more powerful in this situation?"

I decided one thing I could do instantly would be to ask Tyler's advice about shopping. "Do you think Snoopy (our dog) would like this kind of dog food or that kind?" "What vegetables do you think Dad would like?" "How many cans of soup should we buy?" By the time we moved into the next aisle, I was amazed at how cooperative Tyler had become. I thought someone had swapped children with me but I realized it was me that had changed, not my son.

Here is another example of how to give your child appropriate ways to feel powerful.

One mother found herself in power struggles with her three-year-old daughter about putting on her seat belt. She would often arrive at work tense and late from this morning ritual. She asked herself, "How can I give my child more power in this situation?" She thought of a great solution. She decided to make her child the Captain of the Seat Belts. In other words, Mom couldn't drive the car until she got the okay from her daughter (the Captain) that everyone in the car had fastened their seat belts. Her child felt really powerful because she made the decision when they could go.

2. Give your child choices

"Stop that!"
"Hurry up!"
"Get dressed!"
"Brush your teeth!"
"Feed the dog!"
"Get out of here!"

Sometimes our effectiveness becomes diluted because we tend to give commands to our children. The end result of shouting orders is a power struggle between a smug, defiant (or forgetful) child and a challenged, angry adult.

To decrease the frequency of provoking power struggles, give your child choices. Compare the following list of choices to the prior list of commands:

"Would you be willing to play with your truck here without bumping the walls, or would you like to play with it in your sandbox?"

"Would you like to walk with me now, or would you like me to carry you?"

"Would you like to get dressed here or in the car?"

"Would you prefer to brush your teeth before or after I read to you?"

"Would you like to feed the dog or take out the garbage?"

"Would you like to leave the room or do you want me to carry you out?"

Giving choices not only keeps children from becoming dependent upon or rebellious towards authority figures, it also helps them to recognize that what happens to them is connected to the decisions they are making.

Keep in mind these cautions when giving choices.

1. Be sure that <u>you</u> are willing to accept either choice that <u>you</u> give.

2. If your first choice, "Would you like to play carefully in here, or would you like to play outside?" is not acted upon and the child keeps playing carelessly, then give another choice that allows you to take action if he chooses to ignore you again. For example, "Would you like to go outside, or would you like me to take you out?"

3. If you give a choice and the child stalls without choosing one alternative or the other, then assume that he does not want the freedom to choose. You then choose for him. For example, you ask, "Would you like to leave the room, or would you like me to help you out?" If the child pauses

without answering, then you should assume that he does not want to choose and lovingly help him out of the room.

4. Be sure your choice is not a punishment in disguise. One father came to RCB class after discussing choices with his child claiming, "I tried that choice business and it didn't work." I asked, "What choice did you give?" He said, "I told him that he could either stop riding his bike across the lawn or I would beat his @#*'! head in!"

Sometimes it takes practice to get used to giving effective choices, but if you persist the benefits are great.

A mother of two daughters was hosting a series of meetings that I was attending. Her older daughter, Dawn, was seven and arrived home from school during the time our meeting was in progress. Usually, she would walk into the room as soon as she got home and start bothering her mother and interrupting the meetings. Mom was unhappy with what was happening and decided to try a new approach. The next time Dawn came in, Mom gave her a choice. "I'm having a meeting. Would you like to play in your room or in the basement?" Dawn ignored Mom's request and continued talking about what she had done at school. Mom added more firmness, assuming that Dawn did not want to choose for herself, she gave her a second choice. "Would you like to go downstairs by yourself or would you like me to walk down with you?" Dawn again ignored Mom's request and continued talking about school. Mom got up and walked across the room towards Dawn. Dawn stopped talking about school and tried to make Mom feel guilty. "I only wanted to ask you if I could go over to my friend's house! You always told me to ask first." Mom firmly and lovingly continued walking Dawn towards the stairs and helped her go down the stairs. When Mom came back up, Dawn began yelling at the bottom of the stairs, "If you don't come down here, I'll spill my drink all over the floor!" Mom looked questioningly at me, "Now what should I do?" I asked her, "Will the drink hurt the floor?

"Mom shook her head, "No it's a tile floor." So I suggested, "Then don't do anything. Work on one problem at a time."

For the next week, Dawn's Mom continued working on only one problem: Dawn interrupting the meetings. Each week there was more cooperation from Dawn and by the fourth week, Dawn came home, looked into the room, waved quickly to her Mom and went to her room to play. On another occasion, Dawn came home with a friend and as they came into the house, she turned to her friend and said, "Shhh. Mom's having a meeting." The two girls tiptoed through the room to the back door and played quietly in the yard until after the meeting.

About three months later, we met again at Dawn's house. Because it was a long meeting we had ordered hamburgers. When Dawn came home, she saw all the wrappers and empty cups sitting on TV trays and cleaned it up on her own.

Mom had redirected Dawn's old need for undue attention to the new goal of feeling worthwhile by being helpful.

Many parents cite bedtimes as a real source of power struggles. Try giving choices here too. Instead of saying, "It's time for bed," which seems to automatically start the power struggle, ask the child which book he wants read, the story about the engine or the story about the bear? Or instead of saying, "It's time to brush your teeth," ask which toothpaste he wants to use, the white one or the green one.

The more choices you give your child, the more he will feel powerful that he has a say in what happens to him, and the less likely he will feel the need to get into power struggles with you.

Many doctors have taken the RCB course, and as a result have started giving their young patients choices with great success. If a child needs a shot, the doctor or nurse asks which arm she wants the shot in or they will ask which nurse they want to administer the shot. Another choice is, "Do you want a dinosaur bandaid or a turtles bandaid?" Choices like these make doctor visits less stressful for everyone.

One mother even let her three-year-old determine what color to paint the living room! The Mother picked two paint samples, both of which she liked and then asked her daughter, "Angie, I'm debating about the color to paint the living room. Would you pick which color you think it should be?" Mom said that when her friends came over, she would make sure Angie overheard her say that Angie had picked the color of the living room. Mom said that she could see how proud Angie was of herself for having made that decision.

Sometimes we have difficulty thinking of choices for our children. That difficulty may be the result of you feeling like you don't have many choices in your personal life. You may want to practice giving yourself choices, seeing several options. For example, if you think you have to do the dishes but you don't want to, create some options. You could ask your husband to do them, ask your kids to do them, use paper plates, leave them until the morning, hire a maid, etc. So remember, if you want to create choices for your children, practice creating choices for yourself.

3. Give notice of time

You've been invited to a special party for a visiting dignitary. There are many interesting people to talk to and you are circulating between one stimulating group of people to another. You haven't had so much fun in years! You settle into a conversation with a woman from Russia who is telling you about the social customs there and how different it is for her in America. Suddenly, your husband comes up behind you, grabs your hand, forces your coat on you and says, "Come on. It's time to go home."

How would you feel? What would you feel like doing? Children have similar feelings when we demand that they make an abrupt shift in what they are doing (like going home from a friend's house or going to bed). It works best if you can give them a friendly notification such as, "I would like to leave in five minutes," or "Bedtime is in ten minutes." Notice how much better you would have felt toward your husband if he had said in the above example, "I would like to leave in fifteen minutes." Be aware of how less resistant you would feel with that approach.

4. Help the child feel valuable

Everyone needs to feel they are valuable. The more chances you give your child to feel valuable, the less likely she will misbehave. Here is another example:

A father was having frequent power struggles with his sixteen-year-old son about the family car. One night his son borrowed the car to visit his friends. The next day his father needed to pick up an important client at the airport. He opened the door to the car and two empty coke cans fell out onto the driveway. When he sat behind the wheel, he noticed greasy prints all over the dash, french fries stuck in the cracks of the seats, and half-eaten burgers still in the wrappers on the floor of the car. The final insult was starting the car and noticing that the gas tank was on empty. On the way to the airport, the father decided he wanted to handle this situation differently with his son.

That evening, he sat down with his son and told him that he was in the market for a new car and he knew what a great "wheeler and dealer" his son was. Dad asked him if he would be willing to buy the car for him. Dad carefully described the necessary parameters; it had to be a four- door, get 18 or more miles per gallon and he didn't want to spend more than $16,000.

Within a week, the son got an incredible deal for his father, meeting all the parameters and for less money than his father was willing to pay. But, Dad actually got more than a car of his dreams. His son kept the new car free of trash when he borrowed it, policed other family members who left their trash in the car and on weekends, he often washed and waxed the new car! Why the change? Because Dad decided to find a way for his son to feel valuable and at the same time, develop a sense of ownership about the new car.

Here is another father's story.

A father had a twelve-year-old who was not doing well at school and getting homework completed was always a struggle. After attending the RCB course, Dad decided to do something to make his son feel valuable. He taught his son how to do the payroll for his three employees at his floral shop. By the end of the year, the son was doing the payroll so skillfully, he began doing payroll for two other florists in town. Not surprisingly his grades also improved. Dad had guessed that one of the reasons his son was getting bad grades was to get even with Dad for the lack of quality time they had shared. Since Dad was self-employed and wasn't home much, the time he and his son spent together on the family business improved their relationship. By allowing his son to help him, Dad started really valuing his son and acknowledging him for his help.

Here is another example of helping the child feel valuable.

One day I came home upset about a conflict I had been in with one of my staff members. I had left the office with it still unresolved and it really bothered me. At home, Tyler, who was five-years-old, could see that I was upset and asked me what was wrong. I told him about the situation and asked him if he had any suggestions about what I should do. He thought for a moment. Valentine's Day had just passed and he suggested that I give her one of his Valentine's cards. At first, I criticized the idea in my head thinking how silly to do that. Then I said, "Why not!"

Tyler and I searched through the garbage can and found a Valentine that didn't have too many coffee grounds attached to it. I slipped it in an envelope and put her name on the outside. The next day I went to my employee and said, "I felt so bad about what happened between us yesterday that

I asked Tyler what to do and he suggested that I give you this Valentine." She started crying, I started crying, and we solved the conflict right there. That night, I went home and shared with Tyler what had happened and thanked him for helping me solve my problem. Imagine how proud of himself he felt for being able to help me solve one of my problems at work.

This concept is so important that I am going to give you another example.

One stepmother was having difficulty establishing a relationship with her fourteen-year-old stepdaughter. She decided to ask her stepdaughter to assist her in choosing some new clothes for her husband. She shared with her stepdaughter her lack of knowledge about current fashions and that she would appreciate her advice. The stepdaughter agreed and together they picked out some very nice clothes for her father. The shopping spree not only helped the daughter feel valuable but it also improved the relationship with her stepmother.

5. Use signals

Sometimes when a parent and child are working on resolving their frequent power struggles, it is helpful to have a reminder about this pattern of behavior. One way to remind each other is to develop some discrete signals so that no one is humiliated or embarrassed by their use. Use signals that you both have agreed on and feel comfortable using. Remember that the more power and control you give your child, the more likely he will cooperate. Signals that are funny are also a light way of helping each other. They can be either verbal or non-verbal. Here is an example:

One mom and daughter found that they had too many angry outbursts so they decided they would have a secret signal to alert the other that a power struggle was beginning. They decided that they would pull on their ear lobe as a reminder to the other person that they were using anger to get their way.

Here is another example.

In another situation, a single mother had begun steadily dating a man and her eight-year-old son started "misbehaving". One day in the car with her son, he confided that he was feeling that his mother was spending a lot of time with her new boyfriend and he felt invisible when the boyfriend was around. So they worked out a signal that when the son felt left out, all he would have to say was, "Invisible Mommy" and the Mother would include her son in whatever she was doing. When they began practicing this, it would take the son only a few moments of feeling included to be satisfied that he was important.

After taking the RCB course, one family realized that they we saying discouraging things to each other. So they developed the phrase, "That's a put down," as a signal. Everyone in the family agreed that when they heard that phrase it meant they would start using more encouraging phrases immediately.

6. Make agreements ahead of time

Do you go crazy when you get into the store and your child wants to buy mass quantities of toys? Or when you have an errand to run and the minute you walk in the door the child starts whining to leave! An effective way to deal with this problem is to make an agreement with your child ahead of time. The determining factor of success in making agreements is that you keep your word. If you don't keep your word, your child will learn to distrust you and refuse to cooperate.

For example, if you are going shopping, tell your child ahead of time that you are willing to spend only three dollars (or whatever amount that you are willing to spend) on something special for him and that is all. It works best to actually give him the money. It is also important that you tell your child, ahead of time, that you are unwilling to buy him anything extra. In today's society, it is all too easy for your child to misinterpret commercials and advertisements that lead to the belief, "Love means that my parents buy me things," or "Having things will make me happy."

A single mom owned her own business and would frequently take her child with her to work. As soon as they walked in the front door, the child would start whining about wanting to leave. The Mother decided to make an agreement ahead of time with the child, "We will be here for only fifteen minutes and then we will go." This seemed to satisfy her child and she would sit and draw while Mom worked. Eventually Mom began to stretch the fifteen minutes because her daughter was playing so happily. The next time she took her to the office, she became extremely resistant because Mom had not kept her word previously. When Mom realized this was the reason for her resistance, she began to honor her commitment to leave at the agreed upon time and the child gradually became more willing to go to work with her again.

7. *Legitimize behaviors that you can't change*

One mother had four children who persistently wrote graffiti on the walls no matter what discipline strategies she used. So she wallpapered the children's bathroom with white wallpaper and told them that they could write whatever they wanted in their bathroom. When they were given permission to do that, they decided to keep their drawings confined to the bathroom, much to Mom's relief! Whenever I went to their house, I would use their bathroom because it was a lot more interesting and fun to read!

A teacher had the same problem with kids flying paper airplanes at school. So she devoted some time in the classroom to studying aerodynamics and making the most aerodynamic planes. Much to the teacher's amazement, the students' fascination with paper planes dwindled. For some reason when you legitimize a misbehavior, it makes it less fun to do.

8. Create win/win situations

Most of us were not taught the concept of win/win negotiation. We often experienced win/lose or lose/lose situations. In some cases you win and the other, person loses and in others, you lose and the other person wins. There are other times when you both lose. The most effective negotiations are when you strive to create a situation so both of you win and are happy with the end result. It frequently requires a lot of patience because you must listen intently to what the other person wants while staying committed to what you want.

During this exercise you do not try to talk him into what you want nor do you talk him out of what he wants. You keep thinking of solutions until you both have exactly what you want. Sometimes you are delightfully surprised because you get something better than you expected. The concept of win/win takes time in the beginning to work out, but the rewards are well worth that extra time and patience. The process becomes easier as the whole family develops this skill.

Here is an example.

I was going to do a lecture in my hometown and I asked my son, who was eight at the time, to support me by going along. That night, as I was headed out the door to do my lecture, I happened to look down at Tyler's jeans. There, poking out of a large hole, was my son's knee. My heart sank. I promptly asked him to change. He said, "No" and I found myself engaged in a power struggle. When I noticed I was in the struggle, I stopped to use some of the win/win negotiation skills. I asked my son why he was unwilling to change his pants. He told me that some of his friends were going to be there and EVERYONE who was "cool" wears holes in their jeans and he wanted to be "cool." I told him, "It is important for you to win. I want you to win. However, I will be embarrassed in front of all these people if you have holes in your jeans. How can I win too?" It felt like an impossible situation but Tyler thought for a few brief moments and said, "How about this? How about if I wear a good pair of pants over my jeans. Then, when I'm around your friends, I won't

have holes. When I'm around my friends, I'll take them off."
I marveled at his creativity. He was happy and I was happy!
I said, "What a great solution. I would have never thought of
that! Thanks for negotiating with me."

To summarize, when you are in the middle of a power struggle,
ask your child, "I see how you can win and that's great, because I
want you to win. How can I win, too?" When children see that you
are just as interested in seeing them win as yourself, they are more
than willing to help figure out ways that you both can win.

9. Teach them how to say "no" respectfully

Some power struggles occur because children have not been
taught how to respectfully say, "No." Most of us were not allowed
to say "no" to our parents and when children are not allowed to say
"no" directly, they say it indirectly. They can say "no" by
dawdling, forgetting, doing a job ineffectively so that
you either have to finish it for them or so you don't bother
to ask them again. Some children even get sick. It is much
more difficult to deal with a "no" that is said "under the
table" than one that is said "above the table" (i.e.,
directly). If they can say "no" directly, it becomes a more honest and
clear communication. How many times have you gotten yourself in
trouble because you felt you couldn't say "no"? Allowing your
children to say "no" won't cost you anything because they are
already saying "no" "under the table."

It is important that we teach our children how to say "no". They
are going to need to have that skill to say "no" to peer pressure. As
they get older, it is important to say "no" to drugs, sex and other
situations where someone is coercing them to do something that
would not be good for them. If you don't teach your children, who
will? The pressure to be liked by parents early in a child's life is
probably equivalent to the peer pressure they will feel as a teen, so
what a great place to learn!

In our family, everyone is allowed to say, and be respected for,
saying "no." We also have an agreement that if someone says, "But
it's real important that X happens," then the person who says no will
be willing to negotiate.

For example,

> I'll ask the kids to help clean up the house and sometimes they'll say, "No, I don't want to," and that will be okay with me. Sometimes I'll say, "But it is important to me to get the house picked up because we're having friends over tonight," and then they will pitch in.

As odd as it sounds, allowing your children to say "no" makes them more willing to cooperate. Think about that kind of permission for yourself. How would you feel if you were in a job or a relationship in which you weren't allowed to say "no"? I know I would become resentful of that job or that relationship. In fact, I would probably leave the situation if there was nothing I could do to change it. And our children often leave emotionally, even if they can't leave physically, by becoming distant and non-communicative.

One of the best ways to teach your child how to say "no" is to model it for them. Your "no" may also be phrased as "I'm unwilling to . . .". We must be careful that we don't say "no" in an angry way. Some of us feel we have only two options when we feel like saying "no", "I have to fight or I have to give in". With this attitude, we often tolerate an unacceptable situation until we feel resentful. Then we feel justified in fighting and saying an angry "NO!" We might even attempt to conceal our disagreement with phrases like "I'll see," "Maybe," or "Let me think about it." These postponements only dampen our effectiveness and create doubt about our ability to be assertive. If we say "no" immediately in a kind, but firm tone of voice, it will help our children respect us and make us more effective.

> During a parenting course, a single mother with two children complained that the kids wanted everything. Her daughter Debbie was eight and her son David was seven. "Now, they even want me to buy them a pet rabbit. I know they will never take care of it and I'll get stuck with doing all the work."

After further discussion with the mother, we recognized that she had a difficult time saying "no" to her children. The class assured her that she had a right to refuse, and that she didn't have to fulfill all of her children's desires.

As the weeks went by, it was interesting to see the dynamics of how she would indirectly say "no." The children would ask for something and instead of saying "no," Mom would say, "I don't know. Let me think it over." She would continue to feel the pressure of having to decide and the kids would keep nagging until she felt annoyed. Only then, when she was feeling pressured and angry, did she feel justified in saying, "No. I can't stand you kids constantly nagging me. I've had enough! I'm not going to get that for you. Now leave me alone!" When we interviewed the kids, their complaint was that "Mom never says 'yes' or 'no.' She always says, 'We'll see.'"

At the next class, Mom was excited and enthusiastic. We asked her if she said "no" about buying the rabbit and she said she had actually agreed to buy the rabbit. We asked why, and she explained.

"I didn't say 'no' because after thinking it over, I recognized that I really wanted the rabbit too. But I did say 'no' to the things that I didn't want to do. I told the kids that I wouldn't pay for the rabbit but I would loan them money for the cage and supplies if they saved up enough money to buy the rabbit. I told them that they couldn't have a rabbit if it needed a fenced-in yard because I was unwilling to buy a fence and I helped them make a list of questions to ask the pet store owner. If the answers to the questions proved that they would not be able to take care of the rabbit properly, then I wouldn't allow them to buy it."

"I told them that I was unwilling to feed it, clean it's cage or clean up it's messes, but I would be willing to pay for the food. If they missed feeding the rabbit or taking care of it for two days in a row, I would take the rabbit back. It really felt good to tell them directly what I would or wouldn't do and I think they respect me for it."

.nonths later this was the update.

Debbie and David had saved twenty dollars to buy the rabbit. They took the list of questions to the pet shop and the owner told them that either the rabbit needed a fenced yard or they could get a leash and take it for a walk every day. Mom told the kids that she would not be willing to walk the rabbit. So they agreed to take the responsibility.

Mom loaned them thirty-seven dollars for the cage. Debbie and David did jobs around the house for the next four months to pay Mom back. Without being nagged or re-minded, they did all the feeding and caring for the rabbit. They even decided on their own when the cage needed to be cleaned.

The kids learned to take responsibility and Mom had all the enjoyment of petting the rabbit without having to feel resentful and imposed upon. She learned how to be clear about her boundaries and her own responsibilities. She no longer disturbed the family atmosphere by saying "NO" out of anger and frustration but discovered she could say "no" very effectively.

10. Withdraw from the conflict

Children frequently attempt to defy us. Some parents respond to their defiant behavior by trying to force them to behave or to take "the wind out of their sails." Dreikurs suggests that instead, "we take our sails out of their wind." We have nothing to lose by withdrawing from this type of conflict because even if we succeed in overpowering the child, the child will ultimately feel hurt. As a result, he will try to hurt us back. He may not be capable of hurting us directly, but may get even by doing poorly in school, forgetting chores or with other indirect misbehaviors.

Since it takes two to fight, refuse to participate in power struggles with them. When you find yourself in a conflict with your child, and you feel that it is escalating instead of resolving, withdraw from the conflict. Remember, words said "in the heat of the moment" can be very destructive and slow to repair. Here is an example.

One mother was getting ready to leave a shopping center with her son. He had asked her to buy him a toy and she said "no." He continued asking her why she wouldn't buy him the toy. She explained that she did not want to spend her money on a toy that day. But, he kept picking at her to buy the toy. Mom noticed that she was losing her patience and was about to explode. Instead, she got out of the car (she took her keys with her) and sat on the hood. She waited there for a few minutes until she cooled off. When she got in the car, her son asked her, "What's the matter?" Mom said, "Sometimes I get angry when you won't take "no" for an answer. I like how determined you are and I would also like you to just take no for an answer sometimes." This unexpected, but honest, exchange impressed her son and from then on, he began to accept it when she said "no."

Tips to control your anger

1. Acknowledge that you feel angry. It does not help to stuff or deny your anger. Say how you are feeling.

2. Verbally tell the person what has made you angry. "I'm angry that the kitchen is a mess." Simple as this sounds, this expression alone can help solve the problem. Notice there is no name calling, exaggerating, or blaming involved in this simple statement.

3. Know the early warning signs you experience when you become angry. You might get tense somewhere in your body, such as your jaw or stomach or your hands may start perspiring. If you know these warnings, you can intervene instead of blowing up.

4. Take a "cooling off" break. Count to ten, go to your room, take a walk or remove yourself emotionally or physically from the situation. Do whatever works best for you.

5. After you have cooled off, take the action needed. When you take action, you feel less like a "victim" and you start feeling more in control of your life. You learn to act versus react, which builds your self-confidence.

11. Do the unexpected

Our usual reactions to our child's misbehavior is exactly what our child expects. Doing the unexpected often makes the child's mistaken goal inappropriate. For example, be unimpressed with fears. When we are overly concerned with our children's fears, we teach them to falsely believe that someone will intervene to take away their fear or solve their problem. Being fearful doesn't solve our problems, in fact, it usually incapacitates us. So, our goal should be to help our child work through those fears instead of alleviating them. Even if our child's fear is realistic, comforting him does not soothe him. It actually encourages him to feel more fear.

One father in our RCB class recognized that his daughter was using her fears to get attention. That evening, his daughter started voicing her usual suspicions about unwelcome creatures in her room. She came running into the living room screaming, "Daddy, there's a monster in my bedroom!" Without looking up from his paper, Father said, in a matter-of-fact tone of voice, "Make friends with it," and continued reading. His daughter stood there silently for about sixty seconds, then quietly went to her room. Five minutes later Father went to her room, kissed her, and said, "Goodnight," and nothing more. From then on, she had no more fear of monsters.

Another father, Richard, had an ongoing power struggle with his kids about slamming doors in the house. After trying many ways to get them to stop, he decided to do the unexpected. One weekend, without saying another word to his children, he got out his screwdriver and dismantled all the doors in the house that the kids had been slamming. Richard told his wife, "They can't slam doors that don't exist." His children got the message and three days later, he put the doors back up. There was no more door slamming. In fact, when visiting children would slam a door, Richard would overhear his kids tell the offenders, "Around here, we don't slam doors."

It is amazing how we fail to learn from our mistakes. As parents, we'll continue trying to correct behavior using the same ineffective methods we've always tried and wonder why it isn't working. If we just changed this one pattern by doing the unexpected, it is often enough to make the behavior change permanently.

12. *Make it fun*

Many of us approach disciplining or teaching our children far too seriously. Think about how much more you learn when you are enjoying yourself. Most of the lessons of life should be fun for you and your child. For example, try singing "no" instead of speaking in your usual admonishing voice or try developing a funny character (perhaps Donald Duck) that makes requests to do things, such as household chores.

I was struggling with Tyler over his homework. He was learning the multiplication tables and we were getting nowhere fast! Finally I said to Tyler, "When you are learning something, do you need to see it, hear it, or feel it?" He said that he needed all three. So I took out an oblong cake pan and put a layer of his father's shaving cream in the bottom. I wrote the problem in the shaving cream and Tyler wrote the answer. I was amazed. This child went from one child who couldn't care less about what 9 times 7 equaled to a child who was rapidly writing the answers with as much glee as being in a toy store. And, of course, the homework session ended in an uproarious shaving cream fight.

You may be thinking you don't have time to think of unique ways for your child to learn or that you aren't creative. I urge you to throw out these self-limiting thoughts. It not only was fun for Tyler, but it also became a close bonding time for both of us. And it certainly was better than trying to "pull teeth" by getting it done the old way.

One mom was having a power struggle getting her son to take a bath. As usual, the struggle was getting nowhere. She noticed two squirt guns in her son's bedroom. Grabbing the squirt guns, she yelled invitingly, "Let's have a squirt gun fight in the bathtub!" They both had a great time laughing and giggling in the tub.

This may not be something you necessarily want to try but, the purpose of these examples is to stretch your imagination. Make parenting more fun for you and your child.

13. Slow down!

It appears that the more we rush and are anxious to get things done, the more we put pressure on our children to do things. And the more we pressure, the more resistant they become. Slow down, we don't have time to rush!

Power struggles with a two-year-old

One of the most frequent complaints about ages is that of the two-year-old. We often hear examples in which the two-year-old has been stubborn, defiant, and seems to have only a one-word vocabulary - "no". This age can be very trying for parents. Here is a two-year-old infant saying "no" to an adult who is almost three times his size! This is particularly difficult for parents who feel children should be obedient, or those who place a high value on being in control of the situation, or for parents who are "wishy-washy" or inconsistent about how much they are willing to take.

Examples of stubborn behavior are when a two-year-old throws a temper tantrum after he has been given a reasonable explanation about it being time to go home; or the child who refuses help with a task that he obviously can't handle by himself. Let's take a look at what is happening physically with the child who's engaging in this type of behavior. The child is developing more motor skills. Although he may be a little clumsy, there aren't too many places he can't reach. At two, he is more in command of his speech. With these new-found freedoms, the child is trying to be more autonomous. Keeping these physical developments in mind will make it easier for you to be patient than if you assume the child is deliberately trying to defeat you.

Here are some ways to deal with this behavior:

1. Ask questions that can be answered "yes" or "no" only when you are willing to accept either a "yes" or a "no" answer. For example, tell your two-year-old you will be leaving in five minutes as opposed to asking, "Are you ready to leave now?"

2. Use action rather than trying to reason with your child. Using the example above, when five minutes are up, say, "It's time to go." If your child makes a rebuttal, use action by either picking him up or by walking out the door.

3. Give choices to the child so she can develop confidence in her ability to make decisions in appropriate ways. For instance, give her a choice between two outfits to wear. "Would you rather wear the blue dress or the green jump-suit?" or "Would you like to go swimming or to visit the zoo?"

4. Be flexible. Sometimes the child says "no" and you know that he really doesn't mean it. Be willing to follow through with his "no" choice rather than try to persuade him. This will help your child learn to be responsible for his choices. For example, if you know that Jim is hungry and you offer him a banana and he says "no" in that typical, illogical way, then say "okay" and put the banana away rather than try to persuade him that he really does want it.

*****

The Goal Of Revenge

Terri got caught stealing fifty cents from a boy at school and the teacher sent a note to her parents. Terri's Mother was livid. "Terri how could you do this to us? We would have given you the money. I'm ashamed of you. You have given us nothing but trouble. I just don't understand you. Now, you go to your room. I don't want to see or hear from you until you're sorry for what you have done." Mom gave her a swat on her bottom and led her to her room with a firm grip on her arm.

An hour and a half after Terri came out of her room, she decided to paint her fingernails. She chose a fluorescent pink color and sat down at her Mother's new table, even though Mom had told her many times not to play with nail polish. As she was finishing her nails, she "accidentally" spilled the nail polish remover all over the table, taking the finish off as she tried to clean it up.

When we overpower children, they become discouraged and tend to resort to the goal of revenge. Feeling worthless, disliked, and hurt by others, they want to hurt back the way they feel they have been hurt. Sometimes the revenge may be more blatant than the above example. The child who is extremely discouraged may openly, physically or mentally hurt himself or others.

Redirecting The Goal Of Revenge

It takes a person with patience and understanding to be able to see through the malice that a child in revenge may display. It might help to understand that the hate your child radiates is really how he is feeling about himself. It is important for you to decide that you will end the war and that you will be the first one to quit hurting back. This is difficult because we feel so justified in wanting to hurt back or in wanting to teach the child a lesson. But ask yourself, do you want peace or do you want war? If you decide you are unwilling to quit the war just yet, it is okay. Just realize that your attempts to discipline will be increasingly less effective.

If you choose peace, start by listing five things you love about your child. It is difficult to think about things you love about someone with whom you feel angry, especially when you feel like hurting him back. Thinking about the things that you love about your child will change your attitude from a negative one to a more hopeful, positive outlook.

We suggest that you avoid all punishment. When the child has the goal of revenge, we often feel hurt and are tempted to hurt back. If we retaliate, even though we may temporarily subdue his misbehavior, it will only escalate the problem. Punishment provides him with justification for continued aggression. You won't solve the problem by avoiding retaliation, but neither will you be contributing to making it worse.

The next step is to do something to re-establish a relationship with this child. In more extreme cases of revenge, there may not be any relationship with him because you are both so hurtful to one another that you do not feel like being in the other's presence.

> To follow up on the earlier example, Terri's Mother recognized that she had hurt Terri and made her feel unloved by the things she had said. For two days after the nail polish incident, Mother said nothing about the damaged table. She avoided hurting or punishing Terri. She also spent time thinking about some things she enjoyed about her daughter and mentioned a few of those things to Terri. After the two day cooling-off period, Mother talked to Terri about the incident. "I must have hurt you when I said that you were nothing but trouble. Sometimes I say hurtful things when I don't know what else to do. I'm sorry and have decided to make a centerpiece to cover the spot on the table. Would you like to help me?"

> As a result of this mother's understanding and her determination to end the battle of revenge between the two of them, they were able to enjoy one another as they created a unique centerpiece to cover the damaged table.

When you recognize the goal of revenge, use only natural consequences until you establish a better relationship. Natural consequences are described in detail in Chapter 7. It is too easy when a child is looking for an excuse to get even, for him to misinterpret a logical consequence as punishment. Do not confront this child when you are angry. He will be able to sense your anger and use it against you. Here is another example.

A single mother had a sixteen-year-old son who was supposed to be studying. Instead he was painting a banner for an after-school club to which he belonged. This was a sore spot with his mother because she had been in an ongoing battle with him about homework since school began. Mom started nagging him about the homework. "You promised you'd do your homework before you did anything else. How come you aren't keeping your word?" Her son didn't even bother to look up from the banner. "I will. Now will you quit bugging me?" His Mother gave a sarcastic laugh, "Yeah, I've heard that one before. I want you to stop what you're doing and go in and finish your homework. You'll never amount to anything!" Her son stood up and threw the brush down on the banner and shouted, "Why don't you just leave me alone? I'll do my homework when I'm ready. I'm sick of you telling me what to do!" He stormed into his bedroom and slammed the door.

His mother realized that he was in the goal of revenge and she decided to be the first of the two to stop the battle. First, she remembered the step of doing something to re-establish the relationship, so she quit making supper and asked him to come out of his room. She offered to help him paint the banner and he agreed. They talked together freely for the first time in months and the next morning, he got up early and finished his homework.

Use your feelings as a guide. When you are feeling hurtful or revengeful toward a child, it is a good indication that the child's goal is revenge.

There are two exercises that you can do if you have a particularly difficult child with whom you are working. The first thing you can do is to visualize how you want the relationship to be. Take five minutes in the morning before you start your day and five minutes at night before you fall asleep. Actually see the images, hear the words that you want being exchanged and create the feeling you would like to have when you are around this child. We are told by many sources that humans can create anything they can imagine. Unfortunately, we often imagine the worst - our son getting in an accident or our daughter using drugs. Instead of imagining these thoughts, imagine how you would most like it to be. You may or may not achieve success right away, but be patient.

The second thing you can do with a difficult child is to practice loving him unconditionally. Remember when he was little, it didn't matter even if he threw up on your brand new suit, you loved him anyway! Try practicing loving him unconditionally for a day and if a day is too long, practice for half a day.

One mother had a daughter who was seventeen years old when she decided to leave home and live in an apartment on her own. Her Mother had given her a gas credit card with the understanding that she would be responsible for paying all the bills on the card. Mom got a call from the credit card company warning her that someone had charged $800 on the card in a very short period of time. Mom lovingly got her card back and made arrangements for her daughter to pay back the $800.

Mom said that she was really tempted to not give her daughter any Christmas presents because she was so angry (the incident happened close to Christmas.) However, Mom knew that would be done out of wanting to get even and punish her daughter and it would not improve the situation (but she was tempted).

Three things happened in this incident: first, Mom stayed unconditionally loving: second, Mom did not punish her daughter by taking away her presents; and third, Mom stood up for her rights by taking back the card and arranging payment for the daughter's charges.

⇨⇨⇨

The Goal Of Avoidance

Angie's parents had noticed that she was withdrawing more and more from family activities. Her tone of voice was becoming whiny and she would start crying with the slightest provocation. When asked to participate in activities, she would frequently whimper, "I can't." She also started mumbling words so that it was difficult to understand her. Her parents became extremely concerned about her behavior at home and at school.

Angie began displaying what Dreikurs identified as the fourth goal of avoidance or displayed deficiencies. She had become so discouraged that she was giving up. It was as if she were saying, "I'm helpless and useless. Don't make any demands on me. Leave me alone." Children with this goal exaggerate their weaknesses and they frequently convince us that they are dumb or clumsy. Our initial reaction or response may be to feel sorry for them. You might rarely reprimand this child and at other times you might feel frustrated, because nothing seems to work.

Redirecting The Goal Of Avoidance

Here are some ways to redirect this behavior. It is essential that you immediately stop feeling sorry for this child. When we feel sorry for our children, it encourages self-pity and convinces them that we don't have faith in them. There is nothing that paralyzes people more than feeling sorry for themselves. If we respond to their display of sadness, especially by helping them when we know they can do it themselves, they develop a style of getting what they want by being sad. When this style is carried into adulthood, it is called depression.

Start changing your expectations about what this child can do by concentrating on what the child has accomplished. If you feel that this child will respond to a request by you by saying "I can't," don't make that type of request. The child is working hard to convince you that he is helpless. Make this response inappropriate by arranging the situation so that he can't try to verbally convince you of his helplessness. Be empathic, but not sympathetic. For example, "You seem to feel like you can't do that," versus "Here, let me do that for you. It's too hard for you, isn't it?" You may also say, "Do it anyway," in a loving tone of voice. Arrange for situations in which the child can succeed and gradually increase the difficulty of the activities. Be sincere about all encouragement. This child will be extremely sensitive and suspicious of encouragement and he may try to discount it. Refrain from trying to coax him into doing something. Here are a few examples.

A teacher had an eight-year-old student named Liz, who was using the goal of avoidance. Long after a math assignment had been given, the teacher noticed that Liz had not even started the assignment. The teacher asked Liz why she hadn't started and Liz replied meekly, "I can't." The teacher asked, "What part of the assignment would you be willing to do?" Liz shrugged her shoulders. The teacher asked, "Would you be willing to write your name?" Liz agreed and the teacher left for a few moments. Liz had written her name, but had done nothing else. The teacher then asked Liz if she would be willing to do the next two problems and Liz agreed. This continued until Liz had completed most of the assignment. The teacher had arranged for small successes for Liz by breaking the assignment down into accomplishable tasks.

Here is another example.

Kevin, a nine-year-old boy, was given the assignment of looking up spelling words in the dictionary and then writing out the meanings. His father noticed that Kevin did all he could to avoid doing his homework. He cried and whined and told his father that he felt stupid. Dad realized that Kevin felt overwhelmed by the project and was defeating himself before he even tried. So Dad decided to break the task down into something that was more manageable for Kevin. The first three weeks, Dad looked up the words and had Kevin write down the meanings. After Kevin had experienced success, Dad then had Kevin continue to write down the meanings

CHILDREN'S MISTAKEN GOALS

If you feel:	And the child has these reactions to reprimand:	If the child's actions seem to be saying:	Goal is likely to be:	Corrective measures:	Teach your child to:
Annoyed. Want to remind or coax. Delighted with "good" child.	Temporarily stops disturbing action when given attention.	I only count when I am being noticed or being served. Being loved = having attention.	**ATTENTION**	No eye contact. Use no words. Nonverbally make the child feel loved. Take action as soon as the child annoys.	Get attention appropriately.
Provoked. Need for power. Challenged – "I'll make you do it!" "You can't get away with that!"	Intensifies action when reprimanded. Child wants to win, to be the boss.	I only count when I am dominating, when you do what I want you to do, or when I prove that you can't boss me.	**POWER**	Give choices, not orders. Don't play "tug-of-war." Friendly eye contact. Don't fight, don't give in. Give the child useful ways to feel powerful.	Win/Win Negotiate.
Hurt, mad. You want to get even. "How could you do this to me?"	Wants to get even. Makes self disliked.	I can't be liked and I don't have power, but I'll count if I can hurt others as I feel I hurt.	**REVENGE**	Do not hurt back. Reestablish the relationship. Use logical consequences the child will enjoy. Get close, use friendly eye contact.	Assert feelings of hurt in appropriate ways.
Despair. "What can I do?" Annoyed with pity.	No reprimand, therefore no reaction. Feels there is no use to try. Passive.	I can't do anything right so I won't do anything at all. I'm no good. Leave me alone.	**AVOIDANCE**	Don't coax or show pity. Arrange small successes. Avoid doing for the child. Find situations for the child to feel valuable.	Accomplish and overcome. Feel capable.

(Adapted from an original chart by Nancy Pearcy and Louise Van Vilet) and also look up the first letter of the word in the dictionary, then Dad would do the rest. Dad then alternated looking up every other word with Kevin and Dad continued to break down the task until Kevin could successfully do the whole task without his help. The process took several months to complete, and it proved to be very helpful to Kevin in his school work and to Dad and Kevin's relationship.

IDENTIFYING MISTAKEN GOALS

First example:

In a classroom setting, Mary starts tapping her pencil on her desk. The teacher asks her to stop, but the tapping continues. The teacher snaps at Mary, "I said stop that!" Mary retorts, "No, I won't and you can't make me!"

Questions:

1. How does the teacher feel?

_____

2. What was Mary's reaction to the teacher's reprimand?

_____

3. What did Mary's behavior seem to be saying?

_____

4. What would you guess is Mary's goal?

_____

Second example:

Mary starts tapping her pencil during class. The teacher says, "Mary." Mary stops immediately and says, "I'm sorry, teacher. Do you want me to say all the ABCs now?" "Not now, Mary," the teacher responds. "Wait until your turn." "But I know all of them. Please, can I say them?" "Well, all right," concedes the teacher. "Aaa...Bee...Cee..." Mary's teacher sighs and rolls her eyes as Mary slowly says the alphabet.

Questions:

1. How does the teacher feel?

_____

2. What was Mary's reaction to reprimand?

_____

3. What did Mary's behavior seem to be saying?

_____

4. What would you guess is Mary's goal?

_____

Third example:

During class, Mary suddenly slams her hand down on the desk and jumps to her feet, saying, "This is stupid going over the ABCs. I learned them a long time ago!" The teacher is shocked. She responds by curtly telling Mary, "I'll not have you talking to me that way, young lady. I'm sending a note home to your mother." "Big deal," Mary retorts, "That does it!" says the teacher sharply, "You're going down to the principal's office!"

Questions:

1. How does the teacher feel?

_____

2. What was Mary's reaction to reprimand?

_____

3. What did Mary's behavior seem to be saying?

_____

4. What would you guess is Mary's goal?

_____

Fourth example:

During class, the teacher calls on Mary to say the alphabet. Mary says, "I don't know" and looks down at her feet. "Come on now, Mary," the teacher coaxes, "I know you can say it." Mary shrugs her shoulders. The teacher sighs, then in a gentle voice says, "Come on, Mary, can you say the first letter? Can you say 'A'?" Mary weakly says, "A?" "That's good, Mary," the teacher praises.

Questions

1. How does the teacher feel?

_____

2. What was Mary's reaction to reprimand?

_____

3. What did Mary's behavior seem to be saying?

_____

4. What would you guess is Mary's goal?

_____

Answers:

Example 1:

  1. Teacher feels angry. Her authority has been challenged.
  2. The reprimand was ignored.
  3. "You can't make me."
  4. Power.

Example 2:

1. Annoyed.
2. Misbehavior stops because child received attention.
3. "Notice me."
4. Attention.

Example 3:

1. Teacher feels hurt and revengeful. Feels like hurting back.
2. Mary hurts the teacher again after reprimand.
3. "I want to hurt others the way I feel hurt."
4. Revenge.

Example 4:

1. Annoyed and sympathetic.
2. No reprimand was given.
3. "Leave me alone."
4. Avoidance or displayed inadequacy.

HOW WE ARE MISINTERPRETED

When parents come to the RCB course for help in dealing with their child's behavior, we begin by identifying the purpose for the behavior. Once we have this understanding, we usually recognize that, in response to the behavior, the parents are unintentionally doing things that actually encourage the child to maintain his mistaken goals. The most effective thing that parents can do to improve the situation is to revise the responses they are using that are reinforcing the child to maintain his mistaken conclusions.

In order to do this, we need to be aware of how our child may be misinterpreting our discipline attempts. While Mom is spanking Tommy, she says, "Tommy, how many times have I told you that you shouldn't hit people?"

Mother's intention is to train Tommy not to use aggression as a method of solving problems. Tommy may misinterpret and conclude, "Aggression is necessary. Even Mom uses it so, I guess I just don't have enough power yet."

We know what we are trying to teach our children, but we need practice in recognizing what the child is actually learning.

One evening we were standing in line at a fast food restaurant. In front of us was a father with his three-year-old son. Dad was just starting to place his order when the boy said, in a normal and friendly voice, "Dad." The father ignored his son and continued to place his order. The boy continued with his requests for his father's attention. His voice started to sound whiny and soon the whiny voice became intolerable. Dad finally looked down at his son and said, with exasperation, "What do you want?" The little boy sobbed and motioned that he wanted Dad to lift him to the counter so that he could see. "Oh, alright!" Dad snapped angrily and roughly hoisted the boy to the counter.

Was Dad really trying to give his son whining lessons? If Dad could have recognized what his child was actually learning, then perhaps next time he would be prepared to acknowledge his son's first request (which was, in fact, made in a reasonable tone of voice) or say, "Just a minute, son. I'm busy." Then if the boy persists, he could ignore the unreasonable demands and avoid reinforcing the whining.

Patty's Mother put a lot of effort into doing things so that Patty wouldn't be troubled. She told her when to go to bed so that she wouldn't feel tired the next day. She continually coaxed Patty to eat her vegetables so that she wouldn't get sick. She woke her each morning and often kept calling so that Patty would not be late for school. In short, all the while that Patty was growing up, Mom was a very responsible person.

Now Patty is fourteen and Mom is very concerned. "She doesn't take care of herself," is Mom's complaint. "She stays out too late, doesn't eat right, smokes pot and never brushes her teeth. I can't understand it because I have always taught her how important it is to take care of herself."

It is true that Mom wanted to teach Patty the importance of self-respect, but was that what Patty was learning? It seems more likely that Patty interpreted the help as, "I don't need to take care of myself. That is Mother's job. I can do whatever I please and someone will take care of me."

Patty did not see Mother respecting herself or sticking up for her own rights. Mom was robbing Patty of opportunities to learn from her own experiences. Now Patty is too big for Mom to control and has never had to experience the consequences of her own choices.

If you would like to avoid having this type of a problem when your children become teenagers, ask yourself this question:

"Are my parenting methods teaching my children to recognize that their choices will determine what will happen in their lives? Or, are my methods encouraging them to feel that their well-being depends upon what someone else decides?"

The purpose of this section is to assist you in determining how your child is interpreting the training you are giving him. If you are in a situation where your child is frequently repeating an inappropriate behavior, you can gain insight by asking yourself, "What might I be doing that is encouraging my child to continue this behavior? How might he be misinterpreting me?"

RECOMMENDATION:

Use the goal chart to answer the questions below.

1. What is the behavior I want to redirect?

2. What is the goal of my child?

3. What is the redirection method I will use?

Chapter 3

AUTHENTIC POWER

SOCIAL PIONEERS

A little more than two hundred years ago, a group of coura-geous people who were fed up with the tyranny of an autocratic government, made some political changes that are now having a profound impact on the way we raise our children. The actions of these pioneers gave birth to the United States and to the develop-ment of our present form of democracy.

Although the idea of equal rights through democracy celebrated its two hundredth birthday in this country, the evolution of the attitude of equality that spawned the change has just recently gained enough momentum to have a significant influence on parenting.

As I mentioned in Chapter 1, we see minority groups on every front fighting for equal rights. Most adults are unwilling to accept dictates and children are feeling that same way. In the chart on the following page, there is a list of the characteristics that are manifested when using autocratic and democratic methods. Let's look at the methods that were used to develop those characteristics.

As you can see, there is quite a difference in what is necessary to prepare a child for democracy versus autocracy. Compare these methods of parenting to those which most of us use as a result of our own traditional up-bringing. In the past, everyone knew just what to do to parent their children. But because of today's social changes, we must become adept at using new methods. Our rights have

Characteristics of Autocratic and Democratic Individuals

Autocratic Characteristics	Methods to Develop Autocratic Style
Submissive Dependent Obedient Fearful Follower Passive Tolerant Domineering to Those Under Him Obedient to Those Over Him Lacks Self-Respect Not Very Original or Creative Knows what Is Right and Wrong According to the Leader Lacks Determination	Be Arbitrary Give Few Choices Punish Give Rewards for Doing What the Parent Wants Make Threats Use Fear to Intimidate Criticize Them for Making Mistakes Don't Encourage Them Don't Let Them Challenge Your Opinions Use Comparison With Others So They Will Conform
Democratic Characteristics	**Methods to Develop Democratic Style**
Creative Opinionated Makes Own Decisions Responsible Flexible Can Be Either Leader or Follower Assertive Self-Disciplined High Self-Esteem Respects Self and Others Is Not Afraid to Make Mistakes Promotes Win/Win Situations	Let Them Make Decisions Use Encouragement Help Them Repair Mistakes Give Them Choices Respect Them Don't Pamper Them Let Them Know They Are Accepted Be Firm and Kind at the Same Time Don't Have Double Standards Don't Compare Help Them Learn How Much They Can Do Let Them Help You Seek to Understand Other Points of View

changed and so have the rights of our children and it is time to acknowledge that.

STEPS TO END COERCIVE BEHAVIOR

Another way to view democratic and autocratic methods of motivating a child is to use the words "coercive power" and "authentic power."

Coercive power stems from judging children and situations as "bad" or "wrong" and creating separation. Force is used to manipulate the child to do what the parent wants. It includes the use of guilt, threats, punishment, spanking, sarcasm, criticism, intimidation, humiliation, withdrawal of love, yelling, nagging, or any other attempt to control or force someone to do something against their will. Coercive power motivates through fear instead of love and teaches children to be externally motivated. They look for outside sources to blame for mistakes or to make them happy.

When you coerce your child or others, it may be because you are anxious about something going on in your own life. Perhaps you have just had a conflict with your husband, you have not made time for yourself, you're in a hurry, you're having a conflict at work, or worried about money or a variety of other personal difficulties. Sometimes we coerce because we are preoccupied and aren't peaceful or centered in the present moment. We may have the belief that children must be punished or taught a lesson in order for them to learn to justify our coercion.

When our spouse or child does something that we don't approve of and we use coercive power to change them, they usually respond in an equally coercive manner and the tension escalates. We end up saying and doing things that we wish we could edit out of our lives. The results of using coercive power are revenge, hostility, blame, stress, a lowering of everyone's self concepts, a lack of cooperation and a lack of respect. Ultimately, everyone's aliveness is sapped.

Authentic power, on the other hand, does not judge a child as wrong or bad, but works to unite or bond with the child. Authentic power seeks to understand rather than judge, to love unconditionally, to build positive self concepts and to make sure everyone wins. It is the ability to empower others to become motivated by paying attention to internal feelings, to wants and desires and to listen quietly for inner guidance. Authentic power also teaches children that they are their own source of happiness. It creates closeness, respect, responsibility, cooperation and a sense of joy and aliveness.

Here is an example.

Shortly after my marriage to Brian, I drove four hours to visit my step-daughters. My husband and Tyler had previously gone down. As I drove up, Brian and one of his daughters were getting out of the van and were on their way to the house. I hugged them both and asked, "Where is Tyler?" They told me he was still in the van. I went to the van to give him a hug and was greeted with, "Why did you hug her first?" from Tyler. I said, "Sounds like you need someone to hold you and love you." Tyler said despondently, "Yeah, they don't like me, I hate it here." I affirmed, "When you are at home, you get Dad all to yourself. But when you come here it feels like they don't like you. Sometimes I feel that way, too." Tyler was somewhat relieved that he wasn't alone, "You do?!" I responded by asking, "Why do think they may have a hard time accepting us?" Tyler answered, "Because they might feel like we take their Daddy away." "Probably," I replied while I held him closely. He stayed in my arms for a few moments and then said, "Okay, let's go inside."

Consider how it might have turned out using coercive power as it sometimes does when I'm not feeling encouraged. Using the above example, this is how I might have responded using coercion.

Tyler greets me with, "Why didn't you hug me first?" I would say defensively, "Because I didn't know you were still in the van. Now, hurry up we've got to go inside." Tyler would resistantly say, "I don't want to go in. They don't like me." "Tyler get your shoes on and let's go," I would demand. "I'm not going in and you can't make me," Tyler would pronounce. Exasperated, I would say, "Fine just stay in the van! I'm going in," leaving both of us feeling angry and unloved.

It is so easy to use coercive power because that is how most of us were parented. Yet, it seldom gives us the satisfaction that we are all seeking in our relationships.

The first step in using authentic power is to realize that your child is not "bad" and has not done something "wrong." He is "being" just like you. When you pull your mischief, it is not because you are inherently bad or wrong but because you aren't getting a need met.

The second step is admitting to yourself that coercive behavior is not getting the results that you desire, i.e., more closeness.

The third step is finding alternatives to coercive behavior which are discussed in this book.

The fourth step is to try one alternative and acknowledge yourself if you were successful, and if you weren't, ask yourself how you would do it differently next time.

DO NOT discourage yourself. If you discourage yourself, it will increase the possibility that you will give up and go back to using coercive behavior. Some people are awkward at using authentic power at first because it is new. Do not be too hard on yourself.

The fifth step is to read personal growth books, attend personal growth courses or participate in some type of counseling so that you can unblock your ability to unconditionally love yourself, your child, your spouse, and others in your life.

"WHY WON'T THEY RESPECT ME?"

"Jack, get out here right now and move your bike. It's in my way." "Move it yourself Dad, I'm busy." Jack replied. "When I was a kid," Dad mumbled to himself, "I had respect for my parents."

One of the rights we must give up in order to enjoy the benefits of democracy is the right to demand one-way respect In the previous autocratic setting with the bike, it was important for the father to show who was superior to whom. We grew up being taught to obey our superiors and to command those in lower status. Respect was given only one way - up the ladder towards the more powerful person. In return for that respect, the person of higher status would give charity, if he chose to do so. Mutual respect existed only between those of equal "power" and status.

Today our children feel equal to us and they challenge our demands to one-way respect. Unfortunately, we often unknowingly respond to our children in ways that don't show respect. For instance today's children interpret it as being disrespectful when we:

Shout at them.
Go into their rooms without knocking.
Humiliate them in front of their friends.
Spank them.
Talk down to them (use baby talk).
Kiss and tickle them when they don't want to be.
Hold them down to change their clothes.
Force medication.
Make them eat when or what they don't want.
Use double standards.

Mutual respect is necessary to maintain a democratic setting. If your child does not feel respected by you, it is unlikely that he will respond to your attempts to win his cooperation. Respect from your child can no longer be demanded or expected, it must be earned. The best way to get children to respect your rights is to respect theirs. For instance, if you want your child to knock on your door before entering your bedroom, then show them respect by knocking before entering their rooms.

BE FIRM ABOUT YOUR RIGHTS

When we feel resentful toward our children, it is usually because we are allowing them to somehow interfere with our rights. For example:

Mother and a friend were talking over a cup of coffee. Five-year-old Susie came running up to Mom and said, "Mommy, where are my shoes?" Mother answered calmly, "Upstairs in your room." One minute later, Susie was back, "I can't find them!" Mother started feeling annoyed at being interrupted. Sharply she said," Susie, they're in your room, now go find them!" She thought, "I can't even carry on a conversation with my own friend without being interrupted!" However, Mom didn't stick up for her own rights. Instead she showed concern for Susie.

Mom resumed her conversation with her friend. Susie returned in a few minutes and tugged on Mom's arm, "Mommy, I looked in my closet but they weren't there, either." Again, Mom turned her attention away from her friend and showed concern for Susie's problem, "Now Susie, you've got to learn to put things where you can find them." Susie ran back to her room for another try. A few minutes later she returned to Mom sobbing, "Mommy, (sob) I still can't find my shoes, will you come find them for me?" At this point, Mother has had enough and explodes, "If you interrupt me one more time, young lady, I'll put you in your room and then you'll have plenty of time to find your shoes!"

In the example above, Mother allowed Susie to impose on her right to have an uninterrupted talk with her friend. As a result, Mother felt resentful and finally threatened Susie with punishment. Here is an alternative approach that allows Mom to protect her rights:

As Mother and her friend were talking over a cup of coffee, Susie came in and asked, "Mommy, where are my shoes?" Mother replied, "I'm busy right now. I'll help you find them when I am through." "But Mommy," Susie whined, "I can't find them and I want you to help me find them now!" Mother reached over and lovingly rubbed Susie's back without talking to Susie and without interrupting her conversation with her friend. Susie stood there with a surprised look on her face and finally turned around and walked away.

By using this alternative, Mother's actions were saying: "I respect myself and I won't allow you to interrupt me. However, I do love you." She avoided giving Susie negative attention for being annoying and she protected her rights while maintaining harmony. Mother demonstrated for Susie a model of a person protecting her own rights in a loving, but firm way.

BALANCING FIRMNESS AND KINDNESS

Maintaining order in an autocratic setting requires intimidation, "Do as I say or I'll make you suffer." Often in today's democratic atmosphere, parents will recognize the fallacy of being too firm, but they sometimes respond by becoming too kind. In their attempts to avoid intimidation, they may actually pamper the child. Their failure to provide limits for the child can breed insecurity, because he doesn't know how far he can go with his behavior. Or, it encourages him to feel entitled to do whatever he wants. In either case, your child is not being prepared for cooperative living.

The key to being effective is to balance firmness and kindness. Some of us are too kind and some of us are too firm. Some are both kind and firm, but not at the same time. We are sometimes permissive and allow our children to act inappropriately, and at other times, we become too firm and dominate them. Neither method is productive. However, when we combine the two, they become extremely powerful and effective.

Being kind and firm at the same time sounds so easy, but it's difficult to apply. Often unrecognized, traditional beliefs will prevent us from applying this method. You may want to evaluate some of your beliefs using the following questions.

These beliefs tend to result in a parent being overly firm:

Do you believe that a child must suffer in order to learn?

Do you believe that you must control your child?

Do you believe that your child must be afraid of you in order for you to be able to make him behave?

Do you believe that the child must know that you are the adult, and he is *only* the child?

These beliefs result in a parent being overly kind.

Do you believe that you must let your child do whatever he wants, so that you don't dampen his creativity or curiosity?

Do you believe that you must protect your child and prevent him from having unpleasant experiences?

Do you believe that you must tolerate misbehavior until you just can't stand it any more and only then do you have the right to get angry?

In order for you to be successful in being kind and firm at the same time, your child must be aware of several things:

1. You accept and love him just the way he is.
2. You are not going to allow him to infringe on your rights, nor are you going to make him suffer.
3. You will not rescue him from pressure if he chooses to arrange an uncomfortable situation for himself.
4. You will clearly state what you prefer him to do.

A major obstacle that makes it difficult to apply the concept of being kind and firm is the way we use anger to get things done. Many of us have learned to motivate people by using anger. Sometimes we use anger when we are feeling threatened and out of control. Here is an example.

One mother made an agreement that her kids could eat in front of the TV as long as they cleaned up their mess. The children would forget and Mother usually dealt with this problem by yelling at them or spanking.

Here Mother is being much too firm and teaching her children lessons about coercive power which wasn't her desire!

What Mother could do is:

If the kids break their agreement, then the next time they bring their food into the TV room, Mom could silently pick up the food and return it to the kitchen. She may want to say in a firm, but friendly voice, "Since you broke your agreement about cleaning up your mess, I am unwilling to have you eat here now. You can try again next time." At this point, children might try to get the parent to respond in the old way.

"Aw, Mom, come on, don't be such a meany!" Or they might say, "I didn't make the mess, he did," pointing to his brother.

Parents either give in or get angry when children begin to complain. It is crucial that you neither argue nor explain. Instead, give them an accepting look, or some other friendly gesture, but say nothing. If they persist, leave the room.

Although a child may clean up the mess if you spank or yell at him, the price you'll pay is hardly worth it. You will not only disturb the relationship but you will also provoke the child's revenge. He will be less likely to clean up on his own initiative in the future, because you are assuming all of the responsibility for clean-up now. You are teaching him that he needs to clean up only when forced to do so. The locus of control, again, is external and until the locus is internal, he will not clean up of his own volition. Here is another example of being firm and kind at the same time:

A mother who was taking an RCB course said her nine-year-old son, Ryan, was messing his pants six times a week. She told us that she had tried "everything" without success. She had tried many forms of punishment such as spanking and grounding, as well as rewarding him, embarrassing and humiliating him by having him wear diapers to school, lecturing him, pleading with him and making him clean up after himself.

I researched Ryan's history in order to reconstruct how he had arrived at the conclusion that he could gain significance in such an unpleasant way. I discovered that before Ryan was born, there was a baby who died shortly after birth due to an intestinal obstruction. When Ryan was born, he had the same condition and his doctor operated on him, solving his physical problem. However, the parents understandably continued to be overly concerned about Ryan's bowel movements. It seemed that Ryan misinterpreted this concern and concluded, "I can keep Mom and Dad involved with me through my bowel movements."

Once the purpose of the behavior had been identified, suggestions were made to the parents to make Ryan's behavior ineffective. It was important that their actions be both firm and kind to be successful.

The moment the parents noticed that Ryan had messed in his pants, they were to give him a silent hug. It was essential that it be silent, so that Ryan didn't receive the undue attention he was demanding. Hugging him was also being kind. Their actions were saying, "I love you even though you mess your pants." The parents were also instructed that immediately after the silent hug, they should walk far enough away so they couldn't smell him. Again, they were not to say a word. (In this case, there was no need to clean him up since he was already cleaning himself.) They were being firm and protecting their rights by not having to stay around to smell the mess.

After two weeks of being both kind and firm, the parents reported only two "accidents." Both times were when they had company and felt uncomfortable using this method, so Ryan took advantage of their uncomfortableness. Within six weeks, Ryan no longer messed his pants.

Chapter 4

HELP! MY KIDS ARE FIGHTING AGAIN!

There is probably no activity that evokes more frustration from parents than when siblings fight. Parents try many interventions without apparent success. They are sometimes able to stop the fight that is in progress, but nothing seems to be effective in <u>preventing</u> the fights that will start tomorrow. Or, parents will often tolerate and accept fighting as inevitable. On the scale of all of the problems in our lives, it doesn't seem to be important enough to go the extra mile to discover a new way of being that creates peace. However, when you look at the implications of fighting globally and the conflicting relationships between countries, races and religions, the end result is war. In order to learn what we can do to effectively change children's attitudes about fighting, let's try looking at the ultimate expression of these attitudes . . . WAR.

War does not make sense. When countries try to solve a conflict by seeing who can overpower whom, both sides experience pain, loss of life, loss of property and loss of freedom - far in excess of the value of what either ultimately gains or maintains. Wars may be fought for the purpose of upholding high ideals, i.e., the American Revolution. However, what makes war valueless is the fact that you can achieve what you want in life as an individual or a nation without the use of violence.

The continuation of human life on this planet today is precariously dependent upon the mistaken notion that we must overpower one another. This mistaken belief puts us in a position of protection. Therefore we build stockpiles of tremendous weaponry. Each side may concede that this is a dangerous excess of power. However, while we are talking and planning disarmament, our energy and resources are going into developing more power and protection. Billions of dollars that could be used to improve the world are being spent on excessive tools of destruction which will, hopefully, remain unused until the end of the world.

What human misconceptions must be in effect in order to explain these unrealistic beliefs that it pays to fight or overpower another?

You may think it's a bit extreme to compare war with the way that we deal with our children's fights. However, our children will be the future leaders of the world. Wouldn't it be great if they brought win/win principles into our governments? Below are some mistaken beliefs that we may inadvertently lead our children to believe about fighting:

1. I get what I want by overpowering.
2. I can gain recognition by fighting.
3. Only the more powerful person is important.
4. Others will stop me from fighting before anyone gets hurt.
5. I don't need to evaluate how much it will cost me to fight.
6. I'm not important unless I can do whatever I want.
7. I have to either fight or give in.
8. When I feel hurt, I must hurt back.
9. There is not enough to go around, I have to fight to get my share.

Parents make fighting worse by:

- Taking sides or judging the fight. For example, "Now, Jason, you got to sit in the front seat last time. It's your sister's turn now."
- Using comparisons to motivate, i.e. "I wish you would get good grades like your sister."
- Telling them that they shouldn't feel negative feelings toward their sibling, i.e. "You know you don't hate your sister. You love her. You need to learn how to share. It's not nice to hit. You should know better because you are older. Don't hurt her, she doesn't know any better."

Comments like these only add more steam to pressure cookers.

- Forcing siblings to share.
- Asking a child to give up his own needs for his sibling.
- Having a favorite child.
- When parents fight, they may model hurting back in order to get their way in relationships.
- Yelling at or hitting our children.
- Not honoring and nurturing children's differences. When a child feels that his uniqueness is being honored and nurtured, he feels less competitive with others.
- Trying to make it fair.

We, as individuals, often feel that we can have no influence upon major world events, such as war. We overlook the fact that it is a collection of our individual tax dollars that finances war. Of course, refusing to pay those taxes would not stop war because it would do nothing to change the "war consciousness" expressed above. However, as parents, we have a tremendous opportunity to contribute to peace by dealing with our children's fights in ways that do not elicit more battles and war. We need to encourage values of peacefulness and cooperation. World peace is not dependent on our governments. World peace begins in the hearts and homes of our families. When the consciousness changes in our homes, it will change in our government. Let's consider some of the things we could do to influence children to find alternatives to fighting:

1. **Do not take sides.** Don't give them the reward of feeling significant through fighting. Don't be the judge or referee. Don't punish the guilty and soothe the innocent. If you feel that someone may get seriously hurt, you can silently stand by. If Jack picks up a stick, you can silently take it away without stopping the fight. If you do this in a firm but friendly way, without using words, then the responsibility of resolving the fight is still with the children. You may want to silently and gently guide them outside where the fighting won't bother you or your home furnishings. If you decide to separate the children, send them both to separate areas to cool off.

2. **Bring peace to the fight** by getting down on their level. Touch them lovingly. Look at each of them with acceptance, without judgement or anger. If they are fighting over a toy, wait until they get calm, hold out your hand for the object that they are fighting over and tell them, "You may have the toy back when the two of you have come to agreement about it." Then leave the room with the toy and let them work it out. Don't use intimidation to get them to stop fighting. Avoid using phrases such as, "You are going to drive me crazy with your fighting!" or "If you don't stop fighting, I'm going to lock you in your rooms."

3. **Describe** what you see during the fight. When you describe what you see without judgement, it allows the child to see what he is doing, you bring it to his conscious awareness. When he is aware of what he is doing, then he can choose if he wants to continue the behavior. Children will become defensive if you describe in a judgmental way.

4. **Empathize and understand their anger** toward their siblings instead of denying it or trying to stop it. For example, if your child says, "I hate my brother," respond by saying, "I can understand that you're really angry with Jason right now," instead of, "You don't really hate your brother. It's not nice to say those things." Feelings that are understood and empathized with dissipate, losing their destructive charge. Help him get clear on what he is angry about and encourage him to express that to his brother.

5. **Help them win/win negotiate.** Guide their negotiations. Stress not fighting *and* yet not "giving in." Help the children promote agreement. Guide them to find a way to make sure that they each get what they want. Compromise is <u>not</u> an effective solution. It most often leaves both parties feeling exploited, since each is more concerned with the half he has given up than with the half he has won.

When they quiet down, help them to win/win negotiate. Don't try to win/win negotiate while they are still angry with each other. It will not work. If they start to get angry again, go back to describing and empathizing with them until their anger dissipates and then start the negotiations again. Help the children to promote agreement.

In the following example, Mom demonstrates the first five principles of handling fighting. They are: bring peace to the fight; describe; don't take sides; empathize and understand their anger; and teach win/win negotiation. Jenny and Andrea are fighting over a shirt.

Jenny yelling: "Give it back to me!"
Andrea hitting: "No, I had it first!"
Jenny hitting back: "Quit hitting me! You're ripping my shirt!"
Mom gets down on their level, strokes them lovingly on their backs and describes: "It looks like you two are really angry with each other!"
Andrea calming slightly: "Mom, Jenny took my shirt again without asking."
Mom empathizing: "It is difficult sharing clothes with one another."
Jenny: "Yeah, she won't let me wear her shirt."
Andrea: "Well, you never ask me. You just take it and then you don't wash it. Then it's dirty when I want to wear it."
Mom now starting to teach them win/win negotiation asks: "Well, Andrea, how could you both win? What do you think that Jenny wants?"
Andrea: "She wants me to ask when I want to wear her shirt and she wants me to wash it when I'm through."
Mom: "Is that accurate, Jenny?"
Jenny: "Yeah, she never asks!"
Mom: "So if Andrea asks before she takes your shirt and she washes it when she's done, then you both will win?"
Jenny: "Yeah."
Mom suggests, "Ask Andrea for exactly what you want. What I want is..."
Jenny: "What I want is for you to ask before you take my shirt and I want you to wash it when you are done."
Andrea: "OK, I'd be willing to do that."
Mom: "Thanks for working that out. I think it's great that you are willing to share your clothes with each other."

Note: Notice how much more the children learned by Mom doing a little coaching than if she had said, "Will you kids stop fighting! I'm so sick of hearing it! Now, knock it off!" Or if Mom had just solved the problem by taking the shirt from Andrea and giving it to Jenny.

6. **Let them overhear you telling a friend how well they solved their own problem.**

7. If the fighting is bothering you, **leave the house** and go for a walk. Make sure you do not leave the house in an angry way by stomping off or slamming doors behind you. Do not talk. In other words, do not say, "I can't stand to listen to you two fight anymore, I am leaving." This will only make the children feel bad or guilty or powerful in being able to control you.

> My sister and I used to fight frequently when we were children. Our parents tried several things to get us to stop, such as putting us both in the corner, or making us kiss (Yecch) and make up and even though these methods made us stop fighting, we usually continued to feel angry and resentful towards each other. One day when we were fighting, Mother left the house without saying a word. When we realized she had gone, it made us think of not only how uncomfortable it was for us to be fighting, but also how inconsiderate we were to Mom. As a result of Mother's kind but firm, nonverbal message, we not only quit fighting, but we also cleaned the kitchen while she was gone to surprise her and make up for discouraging her.

This left more of an impact on me than punishment and forced affection did. It didn't make us feel angry and hostile toward each other because it became our choice to stop fighting when Mom left. While Mom was gone, we cleaned the kitchen and became involved in working as a team which brought us closer.

8. **Help them realize the pain and futility of fighting.** Sometimes children get so involved in fighting that they don't realize the damage they are inflicting. By asking these questions, you can

bring to their awareness the pain of fighting. "What does it feel like to fight? Doesn't that hurt?" Be sure that this doesn't sound like the beginning of a lecture, though.

9. **Teach them self-control techniques.** For instance, teach him to take a deep breath in through his nose and out through his mouth, counting to ten and saying to himself, "I will handle this peacefully." Model self-control in handling your own anger, while still expressing your feelings appropriately without hurting back.

10. If you have a child who always gives in, **teach her how to assert herself.** For example, if you have a child who usually reacts by crying when someone picks on her, teach her how to yell, "Stop it!" progressively getting louder until the other person backs off. Have her practice with you while you coach. Or, if you have a child who usually gives in to her sibling, tell her that it is not always best to give in. It will be better for her as an adult to develop the skill of win/win negotiation.

11. **Teach your child how to join in respectfully and joyfully when others are playing.** Sometimes children get aggressive or whine when siblings won't let them join in their play. You may want to role play how to join in respectfully and joyfully if you find that she is continually being left out because she whines or makes demands. Use dolls or animals as tools to demonstrate.

12. **Teach them how to communicate** effectively and honestly by saying "I feel... when you... because... and what I want is..." instead of using outbursts of anger or physical aggression to get what they want.

13. When children express jealousy, **teach them that they are whole and complete in themselves** without having the same qualities as the other person. For example, if Jennifer complains to you, "Mom, I'm not as smart as Nathan," respond by saying, "It is not so important that you are the same. I love that you are different from Nathan. Both of you are smart in your own ways. Why would I want two Nathans?"

14. **Teach them how to trade and take turns.** It is helpful to use a timer to help young children take turns.

15. **Teach them to be responsible for helping the other sibling to feel better** if they have hurt each other. For example, "Eric looks sad. What could you do or say to help him feel better? Maybe you could ask him?"

16. **Respond to tattling** ("Mom, Jared hit me!") by saying, "That must hurt. I wonder how you will handle it?" Children usually tattle to get the other child in trouble with the adult. If the children realize that it won't work to tattle, they will usually quit.

17. **Encourage the child to do his personal best** instead of competing. For example, if Rachel says, "Look Mom, I got all As but Heather didn't," respond by saying, "It looks like you did the best that you could," instead of, "I wish Heather could settle down and study like you do." (See Chapter 5 for more on the subject)

18. **Do the unexpected.** If your children are calling each other names, playfully join in. For example, Josh angrily yells at Andrea, "You're a stupid cow!" Andrea yells back, "Well, you're a stupid monkey breath." Dad after observing a few seconds, says in a light, playful manner, "This is great," and says to Josh, "You're a slimy, green piece of mildewed spaghetti left over in the refrigerator!" He then beckons Andrea to play and says, "Your turn." This continues as everyone takes turns. Minutes later they are all laughing about how creative and funny they're being.

19. Instead of judging the fight, **put them both in the same boat.** For example, if two sisters are fighting over what book is going to be read to them, put them in the same boat by saying, "When the two of you have decided which book you want me to read, come and get me." This keeps you from judging and having to choose one child over the other and teaches them how to negotiate while being responsible for solving their own problems.

Examples of putting them in the same boat.

Crash! Mother went rushing downstairs to find a lamp shattered on the floor. "All right, who did it?" Sarah, pointing her finger accusingly, "Mike did it." "I did not, you liar. You did it!" Mike defended himself. "You know how I despise liars! Now who did it?" demanded Mother. Again both children denied their own guilt and accused each other. Finally, Mother turned to Mike, "You always seem to get into trouble and you're the oldest. You should know better. Now, you clean up the mess and no TV for the rest of the week!"

In most families, it is commonplace that mothers and fathers acquire the additional job of being the judge. It is unfortunate, however, that when they assume this role, they are being ineffective with their children. In the example above, mother inadvertently confirmed both of the children's chosen roles in a negative way. She made Sarah special as the younger child who tried to make her sibling look bad in comparison to her. Mike's role as the older, trouble-maker was also confirmed. In addition, mother has set herself up for revenge from Mike who is probably get angry at mother for taking his sister's side. Undoubtedly, he will eventually get even.

Stop for a moment and speculate. How might these roles be expressed in these children's future adult lives if no intervention takes place? Out of his belief that he is bad, Mike may continue to opt for this position by getting into trouble with the law or getting into trouble in his marriage by cheating on his wife. It is pretty easy to guess what might happen to Mike, but what about Sarah? Would she choose a mate that was her equal or would she have a tendency to choose a relationship where she could be superior? To take this to an extreme, she may even choose someone who physically abuses her, someone who is unfaithful or an alcoholic. In all cases, look how "good" she would be compared to the misbehaving man in her life.

When we as parents, are willing to take on the unpaid job of being the judge, we are also teaching our children to be dependent upon an authority figure to determine fairness. At the same time, we mislead them in their expectations about life. Life is not always fair.

Children with parents who strive to provide fairness often feel, in adult life, that their job is to complain about injustice but that they don't have to take any action to correct it. They have learned that it's someone else's job to do something about the injustice!

When we act as a judge, it stimulates sibling competition. Dreikurs used the phrase "putting them all in the same boat" to describe the intervention that is necessary to combat sibling competition. He stressed the importance of children acting as a unit or a team. Doing this relieves you of the burden of being the judge, jury, and prosecutor. If we use the above example again with Mother putting them in the same boat, it might look like this:

> Crash! Mom goes downstairs and states, "It looks like you *two* had an accident." Both children start accusing each other. Mother puts her arms around both of them and says, "It doesn't matter who broke the lamp, but I'm wondering if the *two of you* would like some help in cleaning it up?" Mom asks. The three of them clean up the mess together. Mom then requests in a friendly tone of voice, "Would the *two of you* be willing to contribute fifty cents a week from now until Christmas to help pay for the lamp?"
>
> "But Mom, that's not fair. I didn't break it!" Sarah complains. "Do you have a better idea?" Mom asks. "Yeah, make Mike pay for it. He broke it," Sarah demands. Mom responds, "I'm not willing to do that. I don't want to take sides. If you have any other suggestions, let me know. In the meantime, I'll deduct fifty cents from both of your allowances."

Right now, you may be saying to yourself, "But that doesn't sound fair!" You don't always have to be fair, but you do need to be effective. In the second example, Mom wasn't making Mike special for being bad nor was she making Sarah special for being "better than" her misbehaving brother. Very often, the troublemaker stops getting into trouble when this method of putting them in the same boat is used. Since his sibling begins sharing in the consequences for "their behavior," he no longer gets that specialness of being the troublemaker. The words "their behavior" are chosen because it is a cooperation between the siblings.

It is amazing to watch the children who are not misbehaving deal with the children who are when they must share in the consequences as a unit. Usually, peer pressure is more effective than any adults' attempts to deal with the misbehavior. A common example of peer control is evident with children who are fighting when parents are driving the car. The parents will pull over to the side of the road and wait until the fighting ends. The fighting usually halts because the kids put pressure on each other by saying things like, "Please stop fighting. You know Mom and Dad aren't going anywhere unless you stop." This is only effective when the parents pull to the side of the road without complaining about the fighting. The minute the fighting begins, say nothing, but take action by finding a safe place to stop your car. Sometimes it helps for the adults to leave the car and go for a walk. This avoids being pulled into the middle of the fight and allows the kids to take full responsibility for ending the conflict.

During summer camp, I was driving the camp van when two campers began arguing. I didn't say a word, but looked for a convenient place to pull the van over. I stopped, got out of the van, and sat down on the nearby hillside. One of the kids came over to me and asked, "What's wrong?" I said, "Nothing is wrong - it's just discouraging to hear arguing. So I'm waiting here until you finish fighting." The boy ran back to the van and sixty seconds later, they all called out, "Come on back, we've solved the argument!" We continued on our trip without any more arguments. On the way back to the camp, another argument started, and as soon as I slowed the van down, the conflict ended.

When we refuse to get involved, we find that the other children are more effective than we are in influencing their peers. It is obvious you can't stop the car during rush hour traffic, or when you are about to be late for work. However, if you arrange to do this training when you do have the time, you can enjoy the results of the training at times when you're in a hurry.

Putting children in the same boat teaches them that they not only need to be responsible for their own misbehavior, but also that they have responsibility when provoking others to misbehave. It teaches them the meaning of "I am my brother's keeper."

To summarize the issue of fighting, the four keys to handling it are: don't take sides, bring peace to the fight; put them in the same boat; and, teach them both how to be responsible for creating a win/win solution.

Chapter 5

EMPOWERING YOURSELF AND YOUR CHILD

"I CAN'T BELIEVE YOU DID THAT!"

"I was really angry at you." . . .
"I felt sorry for Ann." . . .
"I can't believe you did that!"

These are comments frequently heard after doing an experiential technique I use in my classes that points out the effects of discouragement. During the exercise, I have everyone sit in a semicircle. Starting at one end, I ask, "What is something from the class that you have tried so far with your child?" As each person talks, we say something encouraging about that person's story, such as: "It must have taken a lot of courage to try that method with all those people around." My comment is very specific and sincere. However, I don't avoid areas that need improvement. I may ask, "Would you like a suggestion?" or "If you could do it over again, what would you do differently?" As I make this type of comment, most of the people become more and more eager to share their experiences. Everyone seems to be enjoying learning through listening to what other people have done well.

When I arrive at the last two people, I change my response. The group instantly loses its eagerness and willingness to participate. They start defending themselves. Others become resistant and quit talking altogether. The encouraging atmosphere changes to one of caution and mistrust. I ask the group if they notice any difference in the way I responded to the last two people. Suddenly, it becomes obvious to them that the change in the atmosphere occurred because I had begun to use discouragement. I criticized the last two people, instead of encouraging them. I made comments like, "What did you do that for?" . . . "You should have known better." . . . "It'll take you a long time to make up for that mistake." Unknown to the group, the last two people were staged. I had asked them before class if they would allow me to criticize them to help make the point. This exercise vividly contrasts the benefits of encouragement with the damage that is done when we use a critical approach.

The majority of children misbehave because they doubt their ability to "fit in" or belong in appropriate ways. They are discouraged. Think about that for a moment. Don't you have a tendency to misbehave (yell, snap or nag) when you don't feel good about yourself? What good does it do to further criticize a child that already feels discouraged?

EMPOWERING YOURSELF

Take Care Of Yourself

The most important thing that I can tell you in this book is to take care of yourself. Have you ever noticed that on days when you are tired or you haven't nurtured yourself, that you overreact to events or become short with your children? When you are in an airplane, the stewardess explains the safety features of the plane. She tells you, in case of an emergency, put your oxygen mask on first and then put your child's on. That's a good rule for life too. First take care of yourself. Then you will have plenty of energy to be a good parent. Another example of this is, imagine that you have a pitcher that represents the total amount of energy you have. During the day you pour cupfuls of energy on your children, your husband, your work, etc. If you don't have a source to refill that pitcher, the pitcher will run dry. Begin to do things that you really enjoy in order to fill that pitcher back up on a daily basis like reading, exercising, taking long hot baths, or meditating.

Figure out what part of the day is the most stressful for you and take measures to counteract the toll it takes. For example, one father found it extremely stressful to go directly from work to his home where three children, under the age of six, greeted him. So he made an agreement with his family that he would go to the gym and work out before he came home. Going to the gym made him more relaxed and put him in a better frame of mind to be with his wife and children when he got home.

Know your early warning symptoms of burnout. What happens to you right before you are about to crash? My symptom is that I have a feeling of being overwhelmed and knowing this symptom enables me to take measures to prevent myself from burning out.

Also, know what things encourage you so that when you get discouraged you know what to do to make yourself feel better. You may have a certain piece of music that cheers you up, a motivational tape, a passage in a book, or a friend who listens to you or makes you laugh.

Finally, be careful about what you think because what you think today becomes tomorrow's realities. This concept is extremely important. What you think about and dwell upon will translate into how you experience life. I used to believe that things happened outside of me and then I thought about them. But the opposite is actually true. So, one way you can change your life is by paying attention to the things you think about. Don't allow your mind to drift into discouraging thoughts. One way is to replace a discouraging thought with an encouraging phrase or thought. The phrase that I use is: I am limitless in power, peace and love. I keep repeating that phrase until I begin to feel better.

In India, the elephants in a parade could be very destructive because their trunks would wander and pull down poles and do other mischievous things as they marched behind each other. The marchers found that if they gave the elephants something for their trunks to be occupied with, like a short pole, then they were more cooperative. Our minds are like these elephants' trunks. If we let them wander, they can create all kinds of mischief. The encouraging phrase is like the short pole in the elephant's trunk. It helps to keep our minds from wandering to negative thoughts.

Develop The Courage To Be Imperfect

Being afraid of making mistakes is the result of living in a competitive society that honors prestige by pitting person against person. Relief from the constant pressures of, "I've got to get more!" and "I'm not good enough!" comes when we develop the courage to be imperfect. Fear of mistakes paralyzes us and keeps us from trusting our own capabilities. It creates an inertia that immobilizes us from taking even the smallest actions.

Rudolf Dreikurs, M.D., wrote in his book, *Children: The Challenge:*

"The importance of courage in parents cannot be overemphasized. Whenever you feel dismayed or find yourselves thinking, "My gosh, I did it all wrong," be quick to recognize this symptom of your own discouragement. When you try a new technique and it works, be glad. When you fall back into old habits, don't reproach yourself. You need to constantly reinforce your own courage, and to do so you need the 'courage to be imperfect.' Recall to your mind the times that you have succeeded, and try again. Dwelling on your mistakes saps your courage. Remember, one cannot build on weakness—only on strength. Above all, remember that we are not working for 'perfection', but only for 'improvement.' Watch for the little improvements, and when you find them, relax and have faith in your ability to improve further. You can't do it all at once. Each small improvement is a step forward. Each step forward is the source of further encouragement."

Replace Guilt

It is difficult to never be angry with your kids. So why do we put pressure on ourselves to be "super parents." When we do get angry, we spend our energy feeling guilty rather than seeking more effective methods. Feeling guilty is an energy waster. Have you ever solved a problem by feeling guilty? Instead of dwelling on your guilt, think about what you would do differently if it happened again.

Here is an example:

"It was the ninth time I had asked Sara to quit running in the living room. I was getting very annoyed because she seemed to just turn me off. So, I spanked her and sent her to her room until she could behave.

"Now, if it happened again, I would like to ask her once to stop running in the living room. If she didn't respond, I would pick her up gently and take her down to the family room, or I could take her outside. I won't talk to her anymore about running in the living room because she already knows that she's not supposed to run in that part of the house. If I talk, remind, or scold, I'll just be giving her negative attention."

Guilt is completely ineffective. Find alternatives to feeling guilty, because it only saps our self-confidence and doesn't help you avoid making the same mistake next time.

Sacrifice

Usually we think of sacrifice as a noble thing to do. But have you ever considered that sacrifice can be a very hostile action? It becomes hostile when there are strings attached to our sacrifice to make the other person feel guilty. Or, when we become resentful or feel used and unappreciated because we chose to make the sacrifice. So, be careful when you agree to do things. Make sure that they are things that you really want to do. Otherwise, don't do them.

Know What You Want

Sometimes I catch myself just going through the motions of life and then I start feeling empty. One way that I make myself feel good is to figure out what I want and then make it happen. I used to have difficulty figuring out what I wanted, because I spent so much of my life trying to be good and please others. I remember my husband asking me what movie I wanted to see and I would respond by saying, "I don't know. What movie would you like to see?" When I started figuring out what I wanted and going for it, I became a much more confident person. One of the questions I ask myself in dealing with my children or other relationships is "What do I want to have happen from this situation?"

Avoid Being Wishy-Washy

When you are wishy-washy about what you want, your children will take advantage of your indecision.

> When Tyler was old enough to be sleeping through the night but wasn't, I couldn't figure out why. I was working full time and waking up in the middle of the night to nurse him and it was making me very tired. One night as I was nursing Tyler, I asked myself, "What might I be doing to encourage Tyler to get up in the middle of the night?" I realized that nursing him at that hour was the only time in the day when I was alone with him without thinking of anything else and I was really enjoying it.
>
> I decided that I was going to continue for the next thirty days with our midnight rendezvous and then I was going to train him to sleep through the night. I also cleared my schedule over the next month so that I had more time with Tyler during the day. However after thirty days, Tyler "magically" started sleeping through the night.

Our children can read our intentions and since I had made up my mind that I was no longer willing to get up in the middle of the night. Tyler had "read" that intention. So, if you have an issue with your children, get clear about what you want. Your children will pick up on your clarity and determination.

Don't Forget, You Are Human Too

It is important to have the courage to be imperfect. To be effective in today's society, we must be able to take our own errors into consideration without condemning ourselves.

Being human, also means we may have mistaken purposes or hidden agendas that interfere with our ability to be effective.

You may feel overly concerned with making sure your children like you. This will make it difficult for you to be firm because you'll have a tendency to give in. "Well all right, I'll buy you the toy if you stop crying."

You may also feel it's important that you are the one who's in control. This feeling gets you into trouble when children challenge or threaten that need for control. Whenever you try to "make" the child do something, you will usually create a power struggle.

Another personal reason that often interferes with our effectiveness is that we want to feel indispensable. Being indispensable feels very good. Picture yourself saying to your boss, "I've decided to quit." Your boss pleads with you to stay, explaining that the business would not survive without you. Wouldn't that feel good?

Often, we can gain a similar feeling in the process of parenting. At first, we <u>are</u> indispensable to our child. Without our abilities, talents and skilled judgement, our child would not survive. Then, our child begins to take our nurturing for granted and even though his skills are maturing, he has learned just what to do to appear helpless. We often allow ourselves to be drawn into requests for unnecessary assistance in order to avoid the more difficult challenges that are confronting us as adults. It is easier for us to succeed in the tasks of tying shoes, deciding how much TV our kids should watch, and getting children started on time in the morning than it is to start a community improvement project, decide how to spend our own leisure time, or get started on our own dreams.

As we begin succeeding in the process of turning more and more responsibilities over to our children, it is very easy for us to feel as if we have been fired. This throws us into the challenging position of having to find something else to do with our time. We are forced to find new ways to feel worthwhile. It is not easy to give up that tremendous feeling of worth which can come from the job of doing all those things for our children. However, our task as parents is to gradually work ourselves out of that job by allowing our children to experience the successes and failures that will lead them to a feeling of self-reliance.

Life Works!

One morning when my son was five years old, I was driving up a winding road through a large piece of property we had just purchased for holding personal growth courses. The property was rundown and would require a lot of repair before our soon-to-be opening. My son turned to me and said, "Mommy, what's that face?" This was a question he often asked me when I was discouraged so I said, "I guess I'm worried." He asked, "Worried? Worried about what?" I answered, "I'm worried about money." Tyler replied admonishingly, "Mom, don't you know LIFE WORKS?"

What a lesson! We often waste too much of our energy worrying about our children or other matters instead of trusting the process of life. We have never solved a problem by worrying about it or getting upset. Many times it is tempting to worry about a problem before we are sure it is a problem. In most cases, it would be more effective if we postponed our concern until we got more information, so that we knew what action to take.

If you are worried about a problem with your child, ask yourself, "What action can I take toward solving the problem?" Then take that action and trust the process.

Let Go

Letting go consists of doing your best in a given situation and then letting go of the results. We often worry or fret hoping that we can control the results of the situation. But the more detached you are from the results, the more peaceful you will become.

When you let go, you often get amazing results. My father used to be a gymnast. I had wanted to be one too, but didn't choose to follow that desire. When I had my son, I wanted him to become a gymnast. But every time I asked him if he wanted to take lessons, he refused. One day I decided to let go of my investment in him taking gymnastics. After letting go of my personal expectations for him, he asked to take lessons. Warning - you can not let go hoping that perhaps your child will do what you want later on. You have to truly let go of the result and the expectation.

Some people confuse not caring with letting go and this is not the case. You can care very deeply and also trust that by knowing you are doing your best, things will work out. You may not get the result that you wanted, but if you look closely, the situation will work out.

Kids Are Our Teachers

It is important that we respect our children. One of the ways that I create respect for my children is by viewing them as my teachers. My children have taught me priceless lessons about how to play, to love unconditionally, to handle anger more appropriately, to let go of grudges, and to find joy in each day.

Have you ever noticed that when a small child gets angry, he just lets off steam and then it's over? What some of us learned to do with this anger was to stuff it. This leads to depression, resentment and very often physical illness. Young children don't hold grudges. They get angry and then it's over. This is different from adults who hold grudges by withdrawal of love or by remembering the incident for years, digging it up at convenient times to use against another person.

I use my children as barometers to measure my own inner peace. Usually, my kids "misbehave" at times when I'm not experiencing inner peace. So when they "misbehave," I check in with myself (as often as I can remember) and sometimes find that I have been working too hard and haven't taken time for myself. Or sometime it's because I haven't spent quality time with my family.

Another way your child can be your teacher is when you find yourself overreacting to your child's behavior, check to see if his behavior is bringing up some unresolved issue for you. For example, when my son started normal exploration of sexuality, I got overly concerned and upset. What I learned was that it brought up my own issues about sexuality as a child. When I was his age and doing the same exploration, I was discovered and was intensely shamed by my parents. So when he was exploring, it brought up all the unresolved shame for me and I overreacted to his normal exploration.

Or, maybe you weren't allowed to be angry or cry as a child, so when your child exhibits these behaviors, you may try to repress them in her. Take a few minutes now and see if there are any situations in which you feel you are overreacting. Consider these situations that might cause you to overreact: sibling fighting, expression of anger, crying, grades, chores, money, or eating. If you find yourself overreacting to these or other situations, ask yourself, "How was that situation dealt with in my family as I was growing up? What did I learn from how that past situation was handled? What would I like my children to learn from this situation?"

*****

EMPOWERING YOUR CHILD

Honoring The Spirit Of Your Child

Imagine your child's spirit being a brightly glowing campfire that dances and grows with each piece of wood that you feed it. Now, imagine someone pouring sand on the fire. What happens? Depending on the amount of sand and the speed at which it is poured, the flame goes out or fades. It is the same with a child. We dampen or put out a child's flame by nagging, yelling, spanking, being overprotective or controlling, using threats, guilt, shame or punishment. Every time we use one of these methods with our children, we depress their spirits. When children are little, they are full of themselves; they believe they can do anything; they are unlimited. If you ask a group of kindergartners, "How many of you believe you could be a great doctor, scientist or President of the United States?" almost all hands will go up quickly and self-assuredly. But, you ask that question to a group of teenagers, and less than half will raise their hands. And, most adults have long since forgotten most of their dreams. What happened? What put out our fires? Luckily, that flame is very resilient in a child and, when fed the right kindling, dances brightly again.

Every day we encounter hundreds of opportunities to either do things to kindle a child's spirit or to dampen it. In this section, I will discuss several ways to keep that fire glowing brightly.

Genuine Encounter Moments (GEMS)

Dorothy Briggs's description, from her book *Your Child's Self Esteem*:

"A genuine encounter is simply focused attention. It is attention with a special intensity born of direct, personal involvement. Vital contact means being intimately open to the particular unique qualities of your child.

"The opposite of a genuine encounter involves distancing. You do not focus attention immediately, you hold back. You see, but from a distance, avoiding personal engagement. Many parents are with their children physically, but mentally their focus is elsewhere. Togetherness without genuine encounter is not togetherness at all."

Often we're so preoccupied with being adults that we ignore our child's communication to us. Other times we pretend that we are listening, while we continue with our own thoughts. Still other times we listen selectively, hearing only what we want to hear. It is important that you listen attentively. This means that you listen not only to the words but also, to facial expressions and body posture.

The National Family Institute reports:

"The average child in America receives only 12.5 minutes per day in communication with his parents. Of that time 8.5 minutes are spent with the parent in correcting, criticizing or arguing. This leaves only 4 minutes per day for the instruction of values, morals, ethics, attitudes, and self-esteem."

In a University of Iowa study, it was found that the average child gets 432 negative comments per day vs. 32 positive comments (Source: Jack R. Gibb).

These statistics are frightening, aren't they? This is why it is so important to offer your child "Genuine Encounter Moments." GEMs help a child feel acknowledged, important, cared for and valuable. When children feel this way, their need to "misbehave" decreases. This doesn't require hours and hours of a parent's time. It means a few minutes several times a day and it works amazingly well with my children. If I give them a few minutes of a genuine encounter, they will play contentedly for an hour or two.

Mother Theresa of Calcutta said,

"Everybody today seems to be in such a terrible rush, anxious for greater developments and greater riches and so on, so that children have very little time with their parents. Parents have very little time for each other and in the home begins the disruption of the peace of the world."

Many studies have been done with people who are dying. Very few of these people said that they wished they had worked more. GEMs are essential for our families. Within minutes your children will feel listened to, important and loved.

Give Unconditional Love

Every time we punish or threaten, use guilt to control, withhold our love, or spank, we are creating fear in our children. Fear destroys children's spirits and makes them feel they are not "good enough." As adults we certainly have enough of that feeling in our own lives to understand how destructive it can be. Our children need to feel unconditionally loved by us; they need to feel that there is nothing they have to do, like get good grades or clean their rooms, to earn our love. Many of us are still striving to be loved for our "doingness" or "busyness" in our adult lives. Ask yourself, "Am I motivating my child through fear or love?"

Unconditional love is essential in raising self-confident children who love themselves, others and the world in which they live.

Using fear to motivate causes children to protect themselves from responsibility by lying and blaming others. Most children react to fear by "fight or flight". They either become rebellious and resistant (fight) or they go away (flight). Fear breeds competition, fighting, separateness, hostility, "uncenteredness" and a focus on scarcity. Fear of punishment causes children to give up who they are and become what someone else wants them to be. Or they give up who they are to rebel <u>against</u> what someone else wants.

Only by giving our children unconditional love will they be free to be the best that they can be and have the ability to encourage others to be their best. It is through unconditional love that we give our children one of the most valuable gifts we can...the ability to maintain their childlike faith in life.

Act, Don't Yak

Did you know that the average parent makes over 2000 compliance requests a day to children? What is a compliance request? It is a request to comply or yield to a command. It sounds like this: "Get up. It's time for school. Get dressed. Eat your breakfast. Put your dishes away. Brush your teeth. Brush your hair. Feed the dog. Pack your lunch. Don't forget your homework. Don't forget your lunch. Pick up your shoes. Pick up your toys. Turn off the TV. Set the table. Do your homework. Take a bath." The list goes on and on. With this constant harangue, wouldn't you "turn a deaf ear?!" There may also be a, "Do it now or you're in trouble" tone to the request. Imagine if your boss did that to you when you went to work! My guess is that you would quickly be looking for a new job. Fortunately, our children can't go looking for a new family. And when they aren't able to verbalize how they feel, it shows up in their behavior. They become resistant, they dawdle or forget or actually put their hands over their ears to shut out the string of commands.

Instead of talking so much, use friendly action. Give your child his comb or his toothbrush with toothpaste on it. Or guide your child to his task by gently and lovingly placing a hand on his back.

Make a checklist with your child of his tasks and if he is too young to read, draw the tasks and have your child put them on the chart. Then go over the checklist with your child at key times during the day so that you aren't bombarding him all day long.

One Mother got tired of nagging and reminding her children to set the table every night. Instead, she decided to take some action. That evening when she finished cooking, she put the food on the table, sat down and silently waited. The kids came in and asked, "What are we waiting for, Mom?" At that point, it would have been easy for Mother to lecture and say, "We wouldn't have to wait if you had done what I've told you to do a hundred times!" Instead, Mother very briefly and casually answered, "Silverware and plates." The kids rushed off and came back with the necessary silverware and dishes and Mother hasn't had that problem since.

Another mother whose children never picked up their dirty clothes without being nagged, stated simply, "From now on, I'll wash only clothes that are in the hamper." She then took action by allowing clothes left out of the hamper to go unwashed. Her children understood the message and made sure dirty clothes made it to the hamper.

Both mothers quit nagging and reminding, which helped them to feel better about themselves and their children. When we spend less time being negative, we can enjoy our children a lot more.

Avoid making frequent requests. Your child may misinterpret the significance of frequent requests and develop the attitude of, "I only have to do what I'm asked to do" instead of scanning the situation and meeting the demands on his own. Repeated requests leave little room for independent action. Your child doesn't feel the responsibility of discovering, on his own how to contribute and be helpful.

When you do make requests, keep them simple; avoid giving lectures or complaining about how he has or hasn't done it in the past.

Do What You Say

It is imperative that you do what you say. When you don't, children learn that parents are all talk and no action and they use that inaction to their advantage. The sooner you take action, the sooner your child will recognize his limits.

Dad and his two-year old son were in a donut shop. The boy was wandering around in front of the doorway. Dad was concerned that his son might hurt himself or become a nuisance to the in-coming customers. He said, "Michael, come here!" Michael seemed to enjoy his act of defiance, and continued to absorb himself in the commotion around the door. Again Dad demanded, "Michael, come here right now or we're leaving!" This one way communication continued for a few more minutes, without any change in his child's behavior. Dad finally picked him up and brought him over to the table. Michael went back to the door as soon as he could wiggle away from Dad's clutches. "Now, Michael, I'm not going to tell you again . . . Michael, get away from that door . . . If I've told you once, I've told you a thousand times . . . MICHAEL! ! !" Dad yelled from his seat at the table.

Dad never did follow through with his promise to leave the donut shop. He didn't do what he said he was going to do. In a sense he lied to Michael.

It would have been more effective if Dad had given Michael the choice of staying beside him or leaving the donut shop after his first request was ignored. If the child hadn't responded to the choice, Dad could have followed through by picking his child up and leaving the shop. Then Michael would have learned that Dad means what he says.

If Dad doesn't want to leave, then he shouldn't give Michael that choice. Whenever you give a choice that you don't intend to honor, you are actually giving a threat. Instead of threatening, Dad could have said, "Would you like to stand over here by me or would you like me to hold you on my lap so you can watch the people getting donuts?" (In this case, both choices are acceptable to Dad.)

Know Your Child

When Tyler is overtired, he gets real irritable and sometimes mean. I know that my best bet at this point is to dispense with any discipline or negotiation and encourage him to go to bed as soon as possible. Other children behave this way when they are hungry. Watch your child's patterns to know when your child is really "misbehaving" or just physically uncomfortable. It is much more helpful if you can get your child's needs met as quickly as possible rather than getting irritated over his behavior.

Don't Major In The Minors

Carefully choose the major issues that are important to you and work with your children on those issues. Don't hassle your child with a lot of minor problems. If you are working on too many issues with your child at once, it can become overwhelming to both of you. It will also prevent opportunities for GEMS.

The One Thing You Can't Teach

You cannot *teach* responsibility, you can only *give* it. I could stand and watch an expert hit tennis balls forever, but unless I am given the opportunity to experience the results of my mistakes and the joy of my successes, it isn't likely that I will develop my tennis skills by simply observing. Likewise, a child will never learn to get herself up on time if we continue to take all the responsibility by waking her everyday. We rob her of the opportunity to experience the consequences of oversleeping when she fails and the pride of self-reliance when she succeeds.

Each month, ask yourself, "What have I done for my child this month that he may be ready to take responsibility for doing on his own?" For example, this month I think I will teach my son how to do his laundry, or I will give my daughter the responsibility for making her own dentist appointment. Make sure these responsibilities are ones you know they can handle. These gradual gifts of responsibility will prove to be far less overwhelming to your child than if you wait until he is sixteen, eighteen or twenty-one and suddenly declare, "You're an adult now - handle things on your own." If you implement this plan, you'll be amazed to see how much responsibility a child can learn to manage and enjoy at even a young age.

Be careful that you give the responsibility in an empowering way. For example, instead of saying, "It is about time you started doing your own laundry," say, "I've noticed that you are handling responsibility really well. I think you're ready to learn how to do your own laundry."

Don't Label Your Child

"I am not what I think I can be, I am not what you think I can be, I am who I think you think I can be." Author unknown.

Think of all the labels for children that you have heard, said or thought.

He's stupid.
He's hyper.
He's shy.
She's a genius.
He's from a broken home.
He's retarded.
She's blind.
He's a teenager.
She's in her terrible twos.
She's pretty.

Labels put children in boxes that make overcoming them difficult. They limit your child both in what she is and what she becomes. As the previous quotation mentions, children are who they think you think they can be. Labels can also become convenient excuses for your child and for you. The result is that your child doesn't have to go beyond his limitations. I was working with a child in a school once and he said proudly to me, "I am hyper!" It was as if he were saying to me, "There isn't anything I can do about it and neither can you!"

Evaluate His Self Concept

There are four major areas that your child considers in developing his opinion of himself. If you understand these, you can do things to help your child be the best he can be. They are:

1. How the parent(s) view him.
2. How his siblings view him.
3. How his peers view him.
4. How successful he feels in being able to accomplish tasks.

If you are aware of these influences, you can evaluate how your child is feeling about himself. If your child is not doing well in a particular area, you can make some form of compensation. One father had a son who was not doing very well academically but he noticed that his son excelled in gymnastics. So, instead of pushing the child in his studies, he concentrated on helping him feel successful in gymnastics. He did not abandon his son's studies, but he focused on what the child did well and encouraged him.

Another mother noticed that her son was getting bullied at school so she enrolled him in Akido, a non-violent form of martial arts. He developed confidence and learned how to assert himself without fighting.

Respect Your Child's Boundaries

It is so important to respect and honor your child's physical and mental boundaries. If we don't respect these boundaries, our child doesn't learn to put limits on how other people will treat her. She may find it difficult to say no to strangers, to people wanting sexual favors, or to others who want to push what they want onto her. She may become promiscuous because she misinterprets sexual advances as how she can get love. The female gender is used here but the same interpretations are equally true for boys.

We invade our children's physical boundaries or space by forcing a child to do things when he doesn't want to do them. Violations include kissing, holding, tickling, forcing medicine or food on them. Entering his room without knocking, and failing to respect his right to privacy are also violations. Sometimes we do insidious things that disrespect their privacy. For example,

James, who was three-years-old, was out with his parents and he had to change his clothes. He wanted to change where people wouldn't see him but there was no place that was private. His Dad tried to talk him out of his need for privacy since he was ONLY three. Besides, why on earth would a three-year-old be concerned about someone seeing him naked? Luckily, Dad caught what he was doing and provided a large towel behind which James could change.

Often, adults will unwittingly violate children's boundaries. A friend of mine remembers when she broke her leg as a child and the doctors cut off her slacks and underpants with scissors. They did this without explaining what was happening or asking her permission to take off her clothes. As an adult, she still recalled feeling scared and violated when she remembered that incident.

Sometimes, it is hard to tell if a child is really enjoying being tickled or kissed. My children and I have developed a signal we use to indicate when they've had enough. Whenever they say the words, "Please stop," then I automatically stop what I am doing because they are no longer enjoying it. By doing this, the children feel empowered by having their boundaries respected.

Another way we overstep our children's boundaries is to violate their mental space by forcing them to tell us things they don't want to tell us, or by criticizing them and not asking their permission to tell things they have told you in private.

Tone Of Voice

Tone of voice is so important in how a child receives your message. Avoid being harsh, short, or demanding and, above all, don't use baby talk. Children feel demeaned when you use baby talk. Use big words and let them ask you what they mean. Talk as if you were talking to one of your friends.

Influence Your Child To Use Positive Self-Talk

You know that voice you have in your head? The voice that says, "You're not good enough." "That was stupid," or the one that says, "You can do it." "Great job!" That is known as self-talk. The messages you give your children at a young age often become their self-talk when they become an adult. Your negative messages later become their discouraging self-talk messages. Encouragement results in positive self-talk and high self-esteem. Be careful what messages you give your child and be aware of how they might interpret what you say. For example, one mother frequently and lovingly called her youngest child "baby." Later, she found out that the term made her child feel small and powerless, definitely not what the mother intended. So check it out with your child by asking, "How do you feel when I....?"

Promote Order And Routine

We enjoy a tremendous amount of freedom with an automobile because we can travel almost anywhere. However, without order and routine, it would be impossible to travel at all. Freedom without order and responsibility is anarchy, because everyone would become a victim of the resulting confusion. As preparation for living in a democratic society, instilling a respect for order in our children is essential.

Our children can be taught to respect and enjoy order by making arrangements to have a schedule that the family follows. This doesn't mean that the entire day should be on a strict schedule or routine. However, you can plan two or three events each week which happen at regularly scheduled times. Your child can then be left with the responsibility of abiding by this schedule. For example, family members may all have busy and varied schedules during the week but, on Tuesday evenings, at 6:30 p.m., the family has dinner together and every member is expected to be there. The food is served at 6:30 p.m. Those who are late, serve themselves. Or on Saturday mornings, from 9:00-10:30 a.m., you can have family meetings and brunch afterwards.

When you have order and routine, it creates a sense of security in your child because he learns he can depend on certain events always occurring.

Honoring Their Intentions

Usually children misbehave unconsciously and aren't aware of their choices. When you bring the "misbehavior" to their attention in a loving way, they can look at their behavior and then choose whether or not to continue.

One of the things you can say to your child in order to take the sting out of a correction and maintain her self esteem is, "You are saying hurtful things and I know that's not your intention."

For example, if your daughter is hurting the cat, you might say, "You are hurting the cat. I know that is not what you intend because you are usually loving to your cat. Is there something you want to talk about?" If you reprimand the child by saying, "Stop hurting the cat!" it is more likely that the misbehavior will just get channeled toward a new victim or continue in some other way.

Empowering Your Child To Decide

It is all too easy for us to make decisions for our children. We think we know best and believe they are not capable of making responsible decisions on their own. Wrong! When an employer hires a manager, one of the most important characteristics they look for is the ability to make decisions. What a gift you can give your child by empowering him to make decisions! Here are some examples.

One mother had an eighteen-year-old son who asked if he could go over to his friend's house at 9:00 p.m. Mom's first urge was to say, "No, you haven't done your homework and it's late." Instead she "bit her tongue" and said, "Think about how much time you need to do your homework and how much time you need for sleep and then decide." Her son decided to go over to his friend's house for fifteen minutes and then come home and do his homework. Mom said she knew that if she had said her first inclination, he would have rebelled and stayed several hours. As a result of turning the decision over to him, he made a very responsible choice. And it took trust and faith for Mom to let him make that decision.

Here is another example of empowering a child to decide.

A woman was visiting her sister before they were to attend a relative's funeral. The seven-year-old nephew asked, "Do you think it would be alright if I brought these candies with me?" The aunt replied, "Think about the situation. We are going to the funeral home which is a very quiet place to say goodbye and be respectful. When you decide what you want to do, let me know." The little boy pondered his dilemma for a few moments and then told his aunt that he had decided not to bring the candies with him.

It would have been much more expedient for the aunt to simply tell her nephew "no". But she took the time to teach him a necessary skill of looking at the consequences of his future behavior and choosing on his own a responsible decision.

One of the things I appreciated about my parents was that when I became a teenager, they didn't tell me what time to be home but would ask me, "What time will you be home?" They honored and respected my ability to make a responsible decision. As a result, I made a conscious effort to never let them down. I knew they trusted me and I didn't want to do anything to betray that trust. I came home on time not because I was afraid of them, but because we shared a mutual respect.

Don't Be

Think of all the messages that we give our children which tell them they shouldn't be who they are.

> "Don't be silly."
> "Be quiet."
> "Sit still."
> "Why can't you be like your sister?"
> "Stop crying."
> "Shame on you."
> "We don't do that in this family."
> "You're so noisy."
> "You're bad."
> "You're being selfish."
> "You're just like your Father!"
> "Don't be sad."

We spend much of the time telling our children not to be who they are and even more time telling them to become who we want them to be. This often results in adults who still do things they don't want to be doing. For example, many adults are unhappily stuck in careers that their parents wanted them to be in.

A father wanted his son to be a dentist. The son didn't want to be a dentist but wanted to be a musician instead. Through a lot of coercion, he reluctantly went to dental school. The other students loved him because he would put dental terminology to music and play it on the piano to help everyone memorize before exams. But after he completed his degree, he gave his diploma to his father and left for Nashville to pursue a career in music!

For this son, pleasing Dad was important, and fortunately he didn't give up his own dreams. However, Dad and he would have had a much better relationship if he had more readily accepted his son's interest in music rather than trying to mold his son into something he was not.

Respect and honor your child's differences. Oneness or closeness does not result from sameness. Synergy comes from inviting full expression of each other.

Help Your Child Trust His Intuition

One day out of the blue, my son asked, "Mommy, why are you mad?" I was caught off-guard and replied, "I'm not angry." Then I questioned myself and realized that I was feeling some anger. I was reviewing a conflict that I had had with an employee earlier. My son's intuition was right and by denying my anger, I was inadvertently teaching my son to doubt his intuition. So I turned to him and said, "You're right, I was angry about a situation at work. Thanks for helping me recognize that."

It is extremely important that we tell the truth about what is going on in our lives, especially to our children. They are incredibly sensitive and knowing. Sometimes we don't tell them the truth in order to protect them. But the problem with that is they know anyway and their imaginings about a situation are often worse than the truth.

A little girl's grandfather died. In trying to protect the daughter, the mother told her that her grandfather had just gone for a long sleep. Soon afterwards, the daughter developed sleeping problems because she didn't want to sleep forever the way her grandfather had.

It is important that we tell the truth to our children about death and other sensitive issues. Talking about our feelings and our relationships with others helps children trust. They know more than we think and we confuse them by telling them things that are untrue.

Don't Deny Feelings

We dampen our children's feelings when we deny their expressions by saying things like:

"You don't really hate your sister."
"How can you be hungry, you just ate."
"Your Mom is only going to be gone for just a few days so there is no need to be sad."
"Big boys don't cry."
"This won't hurt."
"That's not what you really want to do."

Comments like these deny your child the right to feel what he feels. They teach the child not to trust his judgement. And recent findings suggest that if you don't express your feelings, the feelings stay in our bodies and create disease. One reason we may try to repress our children's emotions is that we are uncomfortable with our own feelings. So, being in touch with our own feelings helps us to respond in a more loving, accepting manner.

Teach Your Child Responsibiltiy For Feeling Loved

Often we give love the way that we want to be loved in return. Unfortunately, due to our uniqueness, we may be giving love in a way that the other person doesn't want.

For example, I absolutely melt when someone strokes my hair and I thought my husband would feel that same way. After years of stroking my husband's hair though, I found out that he didn't like it and it didn't make him feel loved at all. What did make him feel loved was when I told him how much I appreciated and admired him. So for years, there had been an unconscious gap in our communication and expression of love.

We can't expect others to read our minds. So it is helpful to teach your children to take responsibility for getting the love they want. One way for your children to develop the skill of getting the love that they need is to have family "love bags". Each family member has a separate bag. Making and decorating these love bags as a family project can be fun. In the bag, you put small strips of paper and on each one you write the way someone can help you feel loved. For example, "Read me a book", "Rub my feet", "Tell me something you love about me", and so forth. Make sure the request can be fulfilled at the time it is made. "Take me to Disney World" would not be a request that could be granted immediately. Requests to buy things are also not recommended. You do not want your child to associate being loved with someone buying her things. When you or your child feels discouraged or unloved, take the love bag to a family member so they can draw from it and fulfill your request.

This is also a great way to circumvent discipline problems. Instead of your child having to "misbehave" to get your attention, he can bring you his love bag and get love in an appropriate way.

You and your spouse may want to have a family bag and a separate bag to use (and savor) just with each other!

Remind Your Child That She Makes A Difference

It is easy for a child to feel like she is "just a child" and that she really doesn't make much of a difference in the world. This is particularly true of teenagers. They tend to feel that the adults have all the authority and what teens think, feel and do doesn't really matter. So remind them frequently that they do make a difference. For example, "You know that advice you gave me about your little sister was very helpful. I tried what you suggested, about not treating her like a little baby, and it really worked."

Support Their Dreams

Find out your child's dreams and aspirations and support him to fulfill them. When you help children to fulfill these dreams, you teach them that attaining a dream is possible. This helps them maintain a healthy attitude about life. Many teenagers and adults have given up their dreams and their lives have become meaningless and dull as a result.

A teenage boy had a dream of playing hockey in the Olympics so his father bought a skating rink that the family could run. He hired a coach and developed a team for his son to play on. Believing in his son's dream and supporting it made his son feel valuable.

I am not suggesting that you give up your own career for your child. But in the example above, it worked out well for the father because he shared his son's passion for hockey.

There are many things that you can do to support your children's dreams. Too often we spend our time working and striving to get ahead. In my counseling practice, I heard many adults complain that their parents never came to their important events as a child and they felt hurt and unsupported.

Teach Them To "Go The Extra Mile"

When our child gets a job done, we are so thankful that she actually did it that we forget to teach her the value of going the "extra mile." It's when you put that something extra into what you're doing. Even if no one else notices, it makes you feel good inside. For example, putting flowers on the table or folding the napkins a special way when you are setting the table, checking over your homework when you're done or sweeping the walk even though you were only asked to sweep the garage. Going the *extra* mile is really an opportunity to feel *extra* good about yourself.

Do Encouragement Feasts Often

An encouragement feast can be done at the dinner table, at family meetings, or spontaneously anywhere, anytime. It is a way to focus on what we love about each other, rather than what is wrong with each other. One way to do this is to put one family member in the middle of a circle. Holding the recipient's hands, each member says, "What I love about you is..." When each member has completed, the person in the middle then says what he loves about himself and chooses the next family member to be in the middle. This continues until each person has had a turn. You'll be amazed at the closeness everyone feels, not to mention the smiles on everyone's face.

Act As If Your Child Can Do It

It's often easier to do things for our child, because the truth is we <u>can</u> do it quicker and more efficiently. But by doing so, we rob our child of the opportunity to learn by experience and to build self-confidence. If your child is trying to put his shoes on and says, "I can't," when you know he has done it previously, smile and leave the room rather than stay there and coax.

By acting as if your child can handle a situation, the child can sense that you have confidence in him and will feel more encouraged to do things beyond what he thinks is currently possible.

Make Sure Your Child Has Responsibilities That Contribute To The Whole Familly

One of the best ways you can help your child feel worthwhile is to provide many opportunities for her to feel helpful. Avoid giving her the "low dignity jobs," such as taking out the garbage and cleaning up the dog's messes. Instead, include tasks such as preparing the family budget, shopping or cooking a meal. Let her know how important her contribution is.

Avoid Shooing Flies

Dreikurs describes shooing flies in the book *Children: The Challenge* as being exasperated by disturbing behaviors which we are inclined to brush aside by saying "don't," "stop that," "no-no," "hurry-up," "be quiet," etc. (just as we would wave aside a bothersome fly). Instead, we need to give the matter our full attention from the beginning, and take immediate action if our request for cooperation is not met. If you say "stop that" and the child continues, then instantly take some action that won't allow it to

.inue. For example, if you have asked your child to quit banging the toy on the table and he continues, gently take the toy away rather than continue to give him the same orders.

Avoid Saying "Don't"

Often we find ourselves telling our children "don't do that" more frequently than we say "you can do it." This is discouraging to our children and to us. Many times we say "don't" over things that really aren't that important. So ask yourself, "Is it more important that I allow my child to explore, or is it more important that I maintain order and control in my house?" Instead of saying, "Don't write on the wall," say, "Walls are not for coloring. Here is some paper."

Avoid Using Comparisons To Motivate

Comparisons breed competition and unnecessary anxiety. When children feel the need to compete it is difficult for them to simply enjoy being themselves. They feel they need to try to prove that they are something different than what they are and, in some cases, give up their own interests in order to attempt to "measure up" to some external standard.

Emphazie Their Personal Best

Teach your child to set his own goals and do his best to achieve them. Ask, "Did you do your best?" instead of, "Were you the best?" or, "Did you do better than someone else?" When your child isn't compared to someone else, he is more likely to enjoy doing his best. This will also help him avoid getting discouraged when someone else is better than him. There will <u>always</u> be someone better than him. Emphasize the "joy of doing" instead of "out-doing." It would also reinforce the value of this lesson if you could model self-acceptance as well.

Encourage Your Child To Give Her 100%

Many of us have learned to "get by" in life. Encouraging your child to put her all into projects and then recognizing the value and the feelings of pride from giving her 100% will teach her that "getting by" isn't enough.

Be Consistent, Follow Through

If you tell your child that you will only wash clothes that are in the dirty clothes hamper, don't give in. Your child won't believe you if you give in and it will be harder to be firm the next time. Also, if you give in, you take on the responsibility that you said you would leave to him. REMEMBER YOU CAN'T TEACH RESPONSIBILITY, YOU CAN ONLY GIVE IT.

Model For The Child

Often we try to tell a child what to do. Sometimes this becomes frustrating to both the parent and the child. Children seem to learn best by adults demonstrating the desired action and then asking the child to do the behavior they have modeled.

Lead Your Child To Accomplishment

Instead of saying, "Here, let me do it," expand on your child's thinking by asking questions that lead him to success. For example, "I noticed last time you did _____ and it worked out well for you. Do you think that might work this time?"

Spontaneous Dissatisfaction

Unfortunately, our spontaneous response to a misbehavior is usually to directly or indirectly indicate to our child that we disapprove of him. Parents frequently communicate spontaneous dissatisfactions like, "Johnny, what's the matter with you? How could you do that?" This impulsively expressed dissatisfaction only confirms the notion that may already exist in our child's mind: "I'm not good enough yet. I don't know how to find a place with useful behavior. When I'm bad at least they notice me."

Resist your first temptation to show disapproval. Instead respond in a way that helps the discouraged child regain faith in his ability. By doing that, we are attacking the core problem (the child feeling discouraged) rather than becoming involved in trying to manipulate the symptoms (the child's inappropriate behavior).

I believe encouragement is so vital to developing a healthy self-concept and establishing family harmony, that this entire chapter is devoted to encouragement techniques.

Use Encouragement Instead Of Praise

Praise keeps your child dependent on the authority figure to feel good (external gratification). On the other hand, encouragement gets her to focus on how she feels (internal gratification).

Use phrases like, "It looks like you enjoyed drawing that picture," rather than "You're a good boy." This gives the child responsibility for his happiness rather than looking for someone or something to bring him happiness. This method helps children recognize that it is their challenge to do things to make themselves happy. Adults who didn't learn this lesson in childhood often disturb relationships later because they expect others to make them happy.

Praise often makes the child more aware of his smallness rather than his capabilities. For example, patting your child on the head or saying, "You're such a good little boy," only accentuates his smallness.

Even saying, "You're such a big boy," can be misinterpreted to mean, "Being older is better, but I'm not there yet." (It is interesting to note that when you ask a child how old he is, he often says, "I'm four and a half years old." Have you ever heard an adult say, "I'm thirty-five and a half years old"?)

Be Specific

Instead of using praise, we suggest that you show appreciation for a child's contributions. Use phrases like, "I appreciated your help with the dishes. It took less time when we did them together," versus, "You were a good girl today." Being specific encourages further cooperation, whereas, "good girl" only communicates a desire to control.

Emphasize The Joy Of Doing

When you want to encourage your child about something she has done, it is helpful to emphasize the joy of doing. For example, when your daughter brings her grades to you, say, "It looks like you really enjoy learning," or "That must make you feel good." Use these phrases rather than phrases like, "I'll bet you were the best in your class," or "You're such a good girl," or "I'm really proud of you."

When you use praise, it is easy for your child to become dependent on an adult's (external) assessment of her. She may feel she has to do things to earn approval. Or she may feel that she must give up if she can't do better than the others.

A woman in her early twenties complained of being depressed. Several months after the death of her father, she dropped out of college and spent the majority of her time lying around the house. During therapy, it became evident that throughout her school years she had excelled. But she didn't excel because it made her feel worthwhile; she did it only to please her father and to make him proud of her. When he died, so did her motivation.

When you use phrases that help your child internalize what makes her feel good, then she becomes more aware that it is her responsibility to make herself feel worthwhile. Children who don't learn to make themselves happy become dependent and demand that others make them happy. They are constantly seeking approval and when they don't get it, they feel rejected. It is as if they feel, "I'll have time to start enjoying life and doing what I want as soon as others are pleased with me."

Look For The "O"

Often when we're angry or defeated by a child, it is difficult to think of something that encourages him. Sometimes you have to really hunt for even the smallest thing to encourage. Dreikurs was a master at this.

An elementary teacher called Dreikurs into her classroom. The teacher proceeded to complain about how awful a child's handwriting was, in front of the child. "Look at this mess. Have you ever seen such horrible penmanship? You can't read a thing on this whole paper!" Dreikurs studied the paper and then smiled at the child. "I don't know . . . that's a pretty nicely shaped 'O' right there," he said, pointing at the only legible letter on the page. His comment proved to be the child's motivation to improve.

It is extremely effective to teach by pointing out what a child has done well. If you try to motivate a child by discouraging or finding fault, she tends to either give up or become defensive.

Use Encouragement Genuinely

A parent tried to encourage her son to stop wetting the bed by saying, "Oh, good boy, you didn't wet this part of the bed." The boy could tell Mom wasn't sincere and really wasn't happy with one dry spot in an otherwise soggy bed. He said, "I'll get that spot tonight!"

Make sure that you don't use encouragement to manipulate. For example, "You're so good at cleaning things, why don't you go and clean your room?" Children can see through insincerity. Avoid using encouragement in a way that sounds phony or manipulative.

Use Your Body

When encouraging your child, let your entire body express how you feel. Look and talk on your child's level. Getting on his level minimizes his feelings of smallness and inadequacy. Get close to him. Don't yell at him from across the room. Put your arm around him or on his shoulder. If that makes you feel uncomfortable, try something similar that makes you feel more at ease. Smile to help him feel accepted or appreciated. These suggestions might seem trite, but it's amazing how little time we take to do these things.

Use Your Shortcomings

Children sometimes feel like midgets in a world of competent giants. They overestimate how much parents can do (some younger children, believe it or not, feel as though parents are perfect) and underestimate their own value and worth. One way to counteract these feelings is to talk about your errors in a positive way. Talking about some of your difficulties and sharing how you resolved these situations helps your child realize that it's important to be open about your problems and what you decide to do about them. By modeling ways of repairing mistakes and handling consequences, you teach your children a new method for dealing with mistakes. They develop the courage to be imperfect.

If a friend asks you for help, you probably respond by being eager for the chance to feel helpful and worthwhile. However, as parents we tend to undermine that feeling for our children by not asking for their help. Take advantage of your shortcomings. Use them to help your children feel worthwhile and drop thinking that children can't help us.

Here is an example of the results we can get when we treat our children the way we would treat a friend:

Shortly before children's camp, we received a long-distance call from a father who had enrolled his two sons in camp. He told us that he had suffered a major financial crisis in his business and he was unable to send his boys to camp.

We had previously met the family at a presentation in their state and had given the parents suggestions on how they could minimize the competition between their two sons. On the phone the father told us they had had excellent results with the suggestions. Both boys were doing well in school. They were really looking forward to going to camp. This concerned the father because he was afraid the boys would regress when he told them that he couldn't afford to send them. He wanted some suggestions on how he could break the bad news to his boys. We suggested that rather than say, "I can't afford to send you," he should elicit their help.

Three nights later, the family phoned us again. The father told us that he had said to them, "Boys, I've made a mistake with my business and lost a big order. Because of this we're going to be very short of money for a while. Do you guys have any ideas that might help me solve the problem?" The father was amazed at the boys' response. "They were the ones who volunteered to give up camp," the father said. He told us that they also suggested that they would start turning off unnecessary lights and both offered to get paper routes and give their earnings to the family. "But," the father reported, "the greatest benefit is that their eagerness to help has made the whole problem less of a threat to me. I feel I have the support of my family. I made a huge mistake, yet the family is closer than ever."

It is evident that the father's willingness to talk about his own mistakes and to ask for the children's help not only avoided a possible crisis, but it also made him feel accepted even though he had made the mistake.

Act As A Filter For Your Child

One of our jobs as a parent can be compared to that of a sieve. It's important that we filter out experiences that would overwhelm our child. It's equally important that we allow challenging experiences to filter in so that our child can learn to be self-confident.

As an example, you wouldn't ask a two-year old, "What do you want to eat this week?" That would be an overwhelming decision for a child that age. However, you may want to ask, "Would you like to have peas or carrots today?" You would be limiting the choices to ones she would be able to handle. She would also develop the feeling that, "What happens to me depends on my choices."

As your child grows older, the choices given should carry progressively more responsibility with the amount being determined by the child's ability to handle previous challenges.

Underestimating

When a child is claiming that he can't do something that he has done before, don't acknowledge his requests to do it for him.

Nate is trying to buckle his shoes. He has done it before, but still insists, "Mommy, I can't." Mother, not being in a hurry, says in a friendly voice, "I think you can handle it." She smiles at Nate and leaves the room.

Mother's tone of voice was very accepting. She wasn't annoyed with Nate. She was telling him that she had confidence in him, both with her words and her actions. We suggest that you leave the room since that makes it easier to keep from coaxing or becoming annoyed.

One of the primary ways we discourage children is to underestimate their capabilities.

One mother was having trouble getting her three-year-old son Adam to come in for dinner. They lived in an apartment building that had a fenced-in playground in the back. Every time she went to get him to leave, it became an embarrassing power struggle. She would end up carrying a kicking, screaming child through the halls of the apartment. Mother decided to try a new approach. The next day she went out to the playground. As she put her arm around Adam, she said. "It's time for dinner." Then, she started walking back to the apartment building. She expected him to follow her, but he didn't. She went up to their apartment anyway and was about to sit down to eat when she heard a knock on the door. There was Adam.

Much to mother's amazement, Adam had not only gotten into the elevator and found his own apartment three flights up, but he had also found a way to get into the building. For security purposes, the building had a door that could be opened only if you had a key. So, this little three-year-old had arranged for someone to open the door for him, gotten into the elevator, pressed the third-floor button and found his own apartment. Mother said that since then she has had no more power struggles over dinner. You wouldn't think a three-year-old would be capable of doing all that, would you?

Sometimes children will use our underestimating to their advantage.

A mother overheard her five-year-old daughter giving her three-year-old brother instructions on how to get what he wanted from Mom. The five-year-old advised, "Ask her when she's in a hurry. Or, ask her while she's on the phone and if that doesn't work, walk away looking sad. Then she'll for sure give you what you want!"

A frequent parental complaint involves getting kids up in the morning to go to school. I recommend that they arrange for their child to get an alarm clock. Occasionally, parents will resist this suggestion by saying that the child will sleep right through the alarm. Ironically, though, these same kids are up on Saturday mornings at the minute cartoons are on TV! Another rebuttal I've heard is, "Our kids don't know how to tell time."

During one of our courses a mother told this story of her (supposedly) naive child.

"I told my two-and-a-half-year-old that I wanted to have an hour to myself between noon and 1:00 p.m. She agreed to stay in her room and nap or play. At first, she came down from her room once every five minutes to ask, 'Mommy, is it one yet?' This defeated my whole purpose for wanting an hour to myself. After much debating, I decided to give her an alarm clock and demonstrate what one o'clock looked like on the face of the clock. So far, so good, I thought to myself. But no sooner had I put my feet up, than I heard my daughter say, "Look, Mommy, it's one o'clock." In her hand was the clock. She was right, it read one o'clock. My two-and-a-half-year-old was not only capable of learning how to tell time, but also how to move the hands!"

Next time you catch yourself thinking that your child isn't capable or wouldn't understand something, re-evaluate. Give your child the benefit of the doubt. You may be surprised!

Make Mistakes A Learning Experience

When your child makes a mistake, don't admonish him. This will only make him learn to cover up mistakes, to lie, or blame others for his actions and be fearful of taking risks in life.

We, as parents, have a tendency to want to protect our children from making mistakes. When they do make mistakes, we often reprimand them or try to solve their problems. Sometimes, we even feel sorry for the child who has made the mistake and, as a result, we console, "It's okay, Mommy can fix it." These methods don't teach our child to be responsible for his mistakes. Making mistakes is essential to learning and an inevitable part of living. It is important to teach children not to hide mistakes, to make excuses or to blame others.

Here are five suggestions that minimize the importance of making the mistakes and maximize the value a child can derive from his mistakes.

1. The next time

Emphasize what can be done next time. Over-concern with what has already happened only encourages excuses and defensiveness from your child. Emphasizing what can be done the next time lays the groundwork for improvement. It also shows your child that giving up or blaming does nothing towards finding a solution to the problem. For instance:

"You're so clumsy. You can't even pour a glass of milk without spilling it!" Or giving a look of disgust for making a mistake. A more effective response would be, "How could you hold the carton so you won't spill the milk next time?"

2. The deed and the doer

Separate the deed from the doer. Help your child recognize that it isn't that you don't like him, but that you're unwilling to accept his behavior.

> "It makes me angry when you do not do your chores," versus "You're a bad boy."

3. Another chance

Give him another chance. This tells your child that you have faith in his ability to improve.

> "You made a mess while eating in the family room yesterday. You may not eat there today, but you can try again tomorrow."

4. Risk an egg

How much does an egg cost these days? Sometimes you might get over-concerned about teaching your child what amounts to an inexpensive lesson and, in the process, our overreaction can impair our child's self-confidence. Often, "risking the egg" pays off because an egg is cheaper than therapy.

> "Jessica would you please put the eggs away?" versus, "No, you can't help put the eggs away. You might break one!"

5. Ask questions

Ask questions that encourage your child to figure things out on his own. Ask in a loving, accepting voice, "What did you learn from that? What will you do differently next time?" "What would happen if . . .?" Do this without imposing a lesson (or lecture) that YOU want the child to learn.

We don't enjoy seeing our children fail. However, we sometimes give them so many instructions to keep them from failing that they end up being confused or they lack a sense of accomplishment because they don't feel they succeed. We often doubt their ability to complete things "correctly" without our help.

A child can be guided in a way that prevents him from failing and, at the same time, helps him improve his feelings of self-reliance. We don't need to make all of the decisions for our children, nor do we need to stand by and watch them grope through failure after failure. Guide them to figure out things for themselves by asking questions like, "What do you think?" and "What would happen if ...?" We can minimize major failures while helping them improve their feelings of self-confidence.

Habits

Another way to encourage is to minimize the importance of bad habits. No habit is maintained unless it has a purpose and making a fuss over bad habits only satisfies the purpose of the behavior.

One father and mother were greatly concerned about their three-year-old daughter's thumb-sucking. They tried coaxing, criticizing, and rewarding and the habit continued. Finally they tried putting hot pepper juice on her thumb. Defiantly, she put it right back into her mouth, glaring at the parents as she continued to suck.

These parents didn't need to work on stopping the thumb-sucking. Their real problem was the power struggle and the thumb-sucking was being maintained by the struggle. Once the parents understood this, they asked her if she wanted to quit sucking her thumb and she said she did. Together, they decided to put a brightly colored bandaid on her thumb to remind her. Each morning she got to choose what bandaid color she wanted on her thumb that day.

Stay Off The Pity Potty

Avoid feeling sorry for your child. It teaches him that an effective way to deal with a problem is to feel sorry for himself. Looking pitiful is an indirect way of asking others to solve his problems for him. This can lead the child to use depression as an adult.

Don't Hover

Avoid overprotection. We all love our kids and don't enjoy seeing them suffer. But hovering over them, as if our task in life was to protect them from suffering any unpleasant consequences, is not helping them.

Although these acts of overprotection will do wonders for our own feelings of importance, they will mislead our children. Overprotection sends the message that life is dangerous and that they need someone to protect them. As our children grow older, that "someone" becomes more and more difficult to find. It also robs them of the chance to develop the feelings that they, on their own, can handle the situations that life presents them. Have you ever watched a bird being hatched? Birds go through quite a struggle to get out of their shells and it is so tempting to help them along by cracking their shell. But did you know, that if you open the shell for him, the chick will die? The same is true of a butterfly struggling to get out of it's cocoon. It seems the struggle gives them the strength to enter life.

One time I invited a friend's eight-year-old son to go swimming. He had chronic ear infections and had to have special ear plugs to prevent getting an infection from the swimming. When we arrived at the pool, he asked me to do it for him since his mother always did it. I smiled and touched his shoulder and said, "I think that you can figure out how to do it." He looked startled and then began to whine and complain that he didn't know how to do it. Instead of rescuing him, I remained silent. He began to struggle with the plugs, dropping them on the ground, and putting them in upside down. Finally, he managed to get them in correctly and the sense of pride on his face was incredible. He had accomplished a task that he could do for himself from then on.

I am not saying that you should never put earplugs in for a child. If we were in a hurry or if I just wanted to do something helpful for him, I would put in the plugs for him. However, by not letting him learn to take care of himself, he would learn to depend on others rather than on his own abilities.

Avoid Humiliation

Sometimes when parents are feeling overwhelmed in their efforts to control a child, they resort to this autocratic technique of influencing by humiliating.

"If you don't stop wetting your pants, I'm going to make you wear a diaper to school!"

"Why do you *always* leave a mess wherever you go? You're such a slob!"

"You're *never* on time. Now tell your friends to go home and you get into the house right now!"

Humiliating a child might get him to do what you want at the time, but it has the side effect of eroding a child's self-confidence and creating feelings of vengeance and mistrust. This is particularly true when we humiliate our child in front of his friends.

(Watch out for using the words *"always"* and *"never."* They are exaggerations and indicate that we are disturbing the relationship. When we feel hurt, we often exaggerate in order to justify the use of excessive retaliation methods such as humiliation.)

It's Not So Important To Be The Same

Avoid comparing. When we use comparisons to motivate a child, she feels that she's not good enough until she measures up. Or she might feel, "What's the use? I can never do that. I may as well give up."

Comparisons breed competition; competition pits person against person. It creates a continuous striving to prove ourselves or to show that we are better than others. There is little time to think about what would make life more enjoyable. I frequently ask parents what they did last week that they enjoyed? Or, what is something that they plan to do next week that they will enjoy? The majority of them have to think for a long time before they can answer those questions.

Parents often ask, "If I don't teach my child to be competitive, how will he be able to survive in this dog-eat-dog world?" The child who has been taught cooperation instead of competition has a much better chance of surviving in a competitive world. He is less dependent on always having to win or being the best. Since those goals are impossible to achieve consistently, the child who is not dependent on being the best is apt to have more realistic expectations of himself. He is also less afraid of failure and isn't easily manipulated by that fear and isn't devastated when something doesn't go his way.

When you're constantly striving to be better, or to prove yourself, you can never be at peace because you never achieve your goal. A friend said to me, "I'll be okay as soon as I get ahead." He was aiming for a moving target that he was never going to achieve.

To help your children avoid this type of lifelong striving, avoid making comparisons. If your child says, "My sister got better grades than I did." Respond by saying, "It's not so important that you and Sharon are the same. Besides, if you decide to enjoy learning, you'll be amazed at how much you can do."

Another way to minimize sibling competition is to stress cooperation and the children's ability to work as a team. "Let's see what we can do by working together. How good are you guys at teamwork?" This redirects their striving away from the goal of trying to outdo each other. Cooperative games are also a helpful way to encourage teamwork.

At our summer camp, one of the cooperative games we played was the Back Bridge. We piled sleeping bags on the ground and had two children lean back to back supporting each other. Then they walked sideways over the pile of sleeping bags. After a few tumbles and discussions about trusting each other, teamwork, interdependence and helping each other evolved into a new skill - cooperation!

Avoid Entertaining

If we entertain our children, they develop an attitude that others should make life exciting for them. A statement like, "I'm bored," means, "I shouldn't have to be responsible for making my life the way I want it to be." The child who is inadvertently taught to feel entitled to entertainment tends to be attracted as an adolescent to activities involving drugs or excessive TV watching. She has learned to be entertained with a minimum investment of her own energy.

So if your child comes to you and says, "I'm bored," avoid the temptation to say, "Well, you could call up Susie or you could finger paint." Instead, say in a friendly tone of voice, "What will you do?" Put the responsibility back on the child where it belongs. If the child asks for suggestions in an appropriate tone of voice (without whining, pouting, or looking sad), then you may want to give an occasional suggestion, but avoid making the arrangements. If your child's tone is inappropriate, you may want to leave the room or ignore the request until she asks in an appropriate tone of voice.

Criticism

Avoid criticizing and pointing out mistakes. Criticism only makes the other person feel defensive and it doesn't help him to learn. When people are afraid of being criticized, they become nervous and uptight. It is difficult to listen and learn when you are feeling tense.

A lifetime of criticism creates a person who is willing to neglect his own happiness in order to be "good enough." This endless striving can be avoided by building a foundation of encouragement before suggesting improvements. A school principal in California requires his teachers to send five children to his office for productive behavior before they can send one for misbehavior.

What Can You Learn From Your Child?

Think of something that you can learn from your child. When you have something on your mind, tell your child. It will help to create an atmosphere of mutual respect.

One mother told her seven-year old daughter, "Judy, it's really neat how, when you're mad, you go into your room and come out a few minutes later ready to talk. I sure wish I could learn to do that." The daughter looked at her strangely and said, "Sure, Mom." Two weeks later, Mom and Dad were having a huge fight. Mom was banging pots and pans and slamming the cupboard doors. Judy came up to her and cautiously tapped her on the leg and said, "Sometimes when I get angry, I go in my room and think happy thoughts. Then it's not so bad when I come out." Mom and Dad caught each other's eyes, their anger melted, and they grinned sheepishly. Needless to say, that ended the fight and also gave Mom an alternative to think about for the next time she got angry.

I Encouraged Her And She Still Didn't Do It!

If you're just starting to use encouragement, don't expect immediate success, "I encouraged her and she still doesn't wipe her feet when she comes in." You may not see a specific change when you begin encouraging but treat it as if you were investing money in the bank. You're not concerned about whether you get something back from your deposit immediately, yet, you know you can reap the rewards later.

It is beyond our imagination what a child could achieve if he is treated with respect and allowed to make mistakes without criticism or humiliation. A child who is responsible for the demands of any situation is one who contributes effectively to loved ones, to his community and to the world.

Parent With The End In Mind

Time and patience now will help your child develop skills that will lead him to a happier adult life later.

For example, if a child has a misdirected goal of power and grows up without any intervention, he may experience many unnecessary adult conflicts. He may have a difficult time finding a mate who is interested in someone who always wants to be the boss. Friends may be scarce because who wants to be around someone who has to have his way all the time? He may even have difficulties accepting instructions from his employer.

We must keep in mind that as parents, it is our responsibility to prepare our children for living in the world as it will be when they become adults. Tomorrow's effective leaders will be those who have experienced democracy as a child and use democratic skills as an adult.

When parents feel hassled in life, they tend to use methods that are the most expedient in order to get the situation under control as soon as possible.

The expedient solution is not always the best solution. Sometimes it gets the job done but, in the long run, it doesn't give your child the lessons he needs as an adult. This is why it is important that you parent with the end in mind; that you ask yourself, "What will my child learn from this form of discipline? Will it foster his self-expression or will it dampen it? Will it help him to develop the characteristics that he needs to become a happy, productive adult?"

In the following chart, the first column has characteristics that would be helpful for your children to possess as adults. The second column lists things that inhibit those characteristics from developing. The final column has the things that ensure that these characteristics will develop.

PARENT WITH THE END IN MIND

ADULT CHARACTERISTICS	DON'T	DO
Team Player	Use Competition or Compare	Promote Win/Win Situations Emphasize the Importance of Making Everyone Successful Have Family Meetings
Internally Motivated	Reward or Punish Make Decisions for Child Praise	Use Self-Quieting Techniques Help Her to Set Her Own Goals Encourage Him
Trusting and Trustworthy	Humiliate Hurt (i.e., Spank) Punish Break Agreements	Keep Your Agreements Allow Him to be Responsible for Something Meaningful
Risk Taker	Overprotect Focus on Perfection Criticize	Teach Her to Repair Mistakes Have a Sense of Humor Regarding Mistakes

Comfortable with Intimacy	Overwork
	Deny Feelings
		Provide Genuine Encounter
		   Moments (GEMs)
		Share Your Own Feelings and
		   Accept Others' Feelings

Prosperous	Focus on Lack
	Tell Your Child You Can't
	   Afford It
		Focus on Abundance
		Have an Attitude of Gratitude
		Brainstorm Ways to Earn the
		   Money

Self-Expressive	Shame Criticize Control Punish	Ask Her Opinion Ask His Advice Encourage Her Individuality

No Limit Thinker	Talk About How It Can't Be
	   Done
	Say "No" Arbitrarily
	Do Things For Your Child
		Give Choices
		Ask Questions That Lead to
		   New Possibilities
		Brainstorm Solutions to
		   Problems

Effective Negotiator	Create Win/Lose Situations
	Be Arbitrary
	Try To Teach Him a Lesson or
	   Make Him Wrong
		Win/Win Negotiate
		Ask Him How He Can Help
		   His Friends or Siblings Win,
		   Too

RECOMMENDATION:

Look for something that you can learn from your child and tell her about it. For example:

"Jennifer, it's really neat how you know all the people up and down the street. We've been living here for three years, and I only know the people next door and the lady across the street. I sure wish I could learn to be as outgoing as you."

Chapter 6

USING CONSEQUENCES TO REDUCE CONFLICT

WITHOUT PUNISHMENT OR REWARD?

Punishment and reward are ineffective methods of preparing children for democratic living. That's because the use of punishment and reward lacks two essential elements needed to be productive in today's society - a sense of responsibility and a feeling of mutual respect. The child who is raised without developing a sense of responsibility is often controlled by others in his adult life. He will usually wait for permission and search out individuals or institutions who will give him orders or he may become a "reverse puppet" by rebelling against society, doing the opposite of what is asked of him. In either case, he underestimates his ability to change things and he doesn't take responsibility to voice his opinion to improve a situation.

The child raised without mutual respect will be prepared for obedience but does not have the social skills necessary for cooperation - which is absolutely vital in a democracy.

IF YOU DICTATE, PREPARE FOR REVENGE

Even though you recognize the futility of trying to "boss" your children, you often resort to dictating because that's the way most of us were raised. A child's usual response to this is to get even. If you notice that your child is trying to hurt you, it may be an indication that you are dictating. Children "get even" with you by talking back, running away from home, getting bad grades at school—the list could go on and on. They feel, "It hurts when you don't value me, so I'll hurt you back."

One day I was working with a mother and her four young children. Mom was complaining that her kids were forgetful. "I tell them to do something and ten minutes later they forget!" When I interviewed the kids, I asked them if there was anything that they would like their mom to do differently. They said, "Yeah, we don't want Mommy to spank us." I asked them, "What do you do to get even when your mom spanks you?" The seven-year old said, "We forget a lot. That drives Mom up a wall!"

I told Mom that instead of dictating, she could talk about "her problem" about feeling overwhelmed at having to do all the work. The family became more responsive to that approach and together they made a list of the chores that had to be done each week. All of them, including Mom, took turns choosing a chore from the list to be responsible for.

Four weeks later they came back to report that chores were getting done without dictating. The seven-year-old added, "It's more fun and we don't have to use our 'forgot power' anymore."

WHY DO WE SOMETIMES SPANK?

You love your children and you want them to be happy and free from pain. Yet on occasion, you might spank them or hit them. Why? It isn't because you are a mean or inconsiderate person because I've never talked to any parent who enjoyed spanking his child. And it isn't because you don't care about them. My guess is that you spank because spanking was what was done to you. And, we often spank because we don't know what else to do. Taking the time to learn new parenting methods can help us to avoid this pitfall.

Also when we experience times when we are intimidated by circumstances or by other people, we are prone to be overbearing with our children. We come home from stressful situations and if our

PUNISHMENT, PERMISSIVENESS, REWARDS AND REDIRECTING

PUNISHMENT REACTIONS

Lying
Blaming
Irresponsibility
Fearfulness
Confusion
Child pleases or resists authority figure
Low self-esteem
External control
Lack of trust
Desire for revenge
Anger displaced on younger siblings
Uncentered children
Sneakiness
Hurtful of self

REDIRECTING REACTIONS

Looks for happiness within
Respects self and others
Consideration of others
Assertive
Internal value setting
Cooperation
Looks to do what is best for
 the situation
Trusts
High self-esteem
Peaceful, calm child
Internal control
Self-motivated
Learns from experience
Makes responsible decisions

PERMISSIVE REACTIONS

Freedom without order
Lack of self discipline and focus
Lack of self confidence
Lack of respect
Child doesn't learn the value of
 contributing

REWARD REACTIONS

Expects and demands that
 others should make him
 happy
Looks for the next reward
Lack of concern for others
Looks to please authority
 figure
Develops the attitude of,
 "What is in it for me?"

children defy us, it amplifies our feelings of powerlessness. So we regain a sense of power by "showing those kids who's the boss." At this point, we often resort to spanking them.

Spanking will not do anything to improve your children's behavior. They may display temporary obedience, but it is usually followed by a subtle act of revenge. In fact, spanking does damage to a child's self-concept and trust in others. Your child then learns to hit or hurt in order to gain control over others and make them do what he wants.

I saw a mother spank her son because he hit his sister to get a toy that he wanted. As she was spanking him she said, "Jeff, you don't hit people just to make them do what you want. Now I don't want to see you do that again!"

Spanking doesn't help our child but it often relieves our own feelings of powerlessness. The simple act of acknowledging that you feel powerless discharges the intensity of that feeling. If we just react and spank, sometimes the guilt compounds the powerless feeling.

Consider these reasons for not using corporal punishment adapted from *Spare the Rod* by Phil E. Quinn.

1. Corporal punishment is unnecessary. There are nonviolent disciplinary alternatives which are even more effective and pose no risk or harm to children.

2. Corporal punishment confuses discipline with punishment. Discipline is used to teach, while punishment is used for purposes of control and retribution. Young children do not commit crimes that require a punishment reaction. Their mistakes call for a corrective disciplinary response.

3. Corporal punishment validates fear, pain, intimidation and violence as acceptable methods of resolving conflicts between adults and children.

4. Corporal punishment preempts better means of commu-

nication and problem-solving. As long as it is an available option, little effort will be made to learn nonviolent alternatives.

5. Corporal punishment confuses the issue of love and violence-teaching that violence can be an expression of love. True love is expressed in much healthier ways.

6. In that all human behavior is symptomatic, corporal punishment merely controls the symptom while aggravating the cause of the personality disturbance in the child.

7. Corporal punishment is dangerous, in that it can escalate into battering.

8. Corporal punishment increases aggressiveness in your child and vandalism in the school and on the street. Violence perpetuates violence.

9. Corporal punishment can result in permanent physical, mental, spiritual or emotional harm to your child.

10. Corporal punishment reduces the ability of your child to concentrate on intellectual tasks,   thereby inhibiting learning.

11. Corporal punishment denies your child a right to equal protection under the law - a right guaranteed to all natural-born citizens of this country in Section 1 of the 14th Amendment to the constitution of the United States.

Next time try this approach. Catch yourself either before or just after you have spanked. Without condemning yourself, ask, "Is there another way I could have handled this situation?"

REWARDS BREED INSECURITY

Rewards interfere with the development of a child feeling

worthwhile. Children may interpret being rewarded as meaning that they don't need to do anything until there is something in it for them. We often feel the most worthwhile when we do something for someone else and expect nothing in return. There is more to life than, "What's in it for me?" In fact, the development of this feeling of being worthwhile is an essential ingredient to good mental health. We often seek security. But we will never find it! It doesn't exist in life. We are always going to be uncertain. We will never know for sure what to expect from other people nor what to expect from life one moment to the next.

The closest we can come to having a sense of security is to develop what Alfred Adler called social interest: feeling worthwhile as a contributor to society and being interested in mutual success. This cannot be achieved if our only interest "What's in it for me?"

Perhaps you recall the news story where people were outraged at a gas station attendant. On a street in front of a gas station, a man's car caught on fire. Flames engulfed the dash board. The driver was frantically using his coat trying to put the fire out. The gas station attendant arrived on the scene with a fire extinguisher and said to the driver, "For twenty dollars I'll let you use my extinguisher." People who have been trained to be helpful only for a price very seldom enjoy the sense of security and well-being that comes from feeling worthwhile.

*****

PERMISSIVENESS

"If it isn't effective to reward and punish, does that mean that we should be permissive with our children?" Tolerating misbehavior is not only ineffective, but is oftentimes harmful to your child. Permissiveness may take the form of not caring about a child's grades, or who their friends are, or where they are, or what time they get home or giving in when the situation calls for firmness. Permissiveness makes the child feel like you don't care and as a result, she may seek care and concern from other people. There are many teenage girls who are so hungry for affection that they end up getting pregnant. Being permissive may avoid conflict at that moment but in the long run it erodes your child's self-esteem.

AVOID MISUSING WHAT "WORKS"

If a child does something he isn't supposed to do and you hit him over the head with a baseball bat, the odds are that he will probably never do it again. So, that's a method that would work, but what works is not always the most effective, especially in the "long run."

Sometimes when we say, "It didn't work," we mean we were unable to manipulate our child to get him to do what we wanted. Ask yourself. "Do I want to control my child or teach him to control himself?"

If we stopped judging our parenting ability by whether or not our child obeys us, we could create more opportunities for teaching. It is more important that a child learns to be responsible to the demands of the situation than it is for him to be obedient to an authority figure. Don't be misled by a child's compliance. Look at the expression on his face, is it saying, "You've got me right now, but wait until you're not looking!"? Or is it saying, "What's the use? There's no chance for me. Who cares?" If you're getting something similar to these expressions, then you are probably misusing what "works."

SELF QUIETING

Parents will often use "time out" as a discipline method but it becomes a punishment when an angry tone of voice is used and you have control over when the child returns. For example, "I'm sick and tired of your whining! Go to your room and stay there until you can behave!" Notice that the parent is sending her child away in anger. The message your child receives is, "I don't like you. I want you to go away so I can be happier." It doesn't teach your child self control when you are in control of when your child returns. When time out is seen as punishment, your child's thoughts are not, "Gee, what did I do and how can I do it differently next time?" Instead, his thoughts are, "This is stupid! I'm angry! Mom isn't fair!" So, "time out" loses its effect when it becomes punishment. Self-quieting, on the other hand teaches internal control and self responsibility.

Self-quieting is what you, or your child can do, instead of reacting negatively to a situation. You or your child can take a break to get into a peaceful state of mind, work through the emotions and find alternative solutions to the problem. It is a way to get calm instead of reacting in an angry or hurtful way.

Help your child create her self-quieting space. This space doesn't have to be in your child's room. It could be a space in the kitchen, the study or, weather permitting, outside. Help your child find things to bring into the space that will help her quiet herself and work through her feelings. Perhaps a tape player with peaceful music, books, play dough, colors, tool bench, or a tree stump with hammer and nails, or other items that will help her work through her feelings to a more peaceful state of mind. You may want to have your child help you to create your self-quieting space. When you model self-quieting for your children, you are giving them the most effective and persuasive lesson of all. A parent may even go with her child to the self-quieting space to model this technique.

Place three questions on the wall in each self-quieting space:
1. What is the problem?
2. What is my part in the problem?
3. What is one thing I can do to improve the situation?

The following is a list of things to do when asking your child to take a self-quieting break:

a) Get on the child's level (i.e. eyeball to eyeball).
b) Be calm and loving.
c) Communicate to him, "It looks like you need a break. Come back when you are ready."
d) If your child does not leave, pick him up or lead him gently and lovingly to his self-quieting space.
e) If your child comes back and acts appropriately, let him stay. If the behavior is not appropriate, take him back to his space without saying anything.

When you tell your child to, "Come back when you are ready," you are teaching your child self-control.

If your child's goal is revenge or power and you begin to get into a battle with him about taking a break then, stop, and you be the one to take the self-quieting break.

It is important that we demonstrate to our children that they don't have to manipulate or consume external situations to get what they want but can turn within to find solutions and peace.

*****

NATURAL CONSEQUENCES

Ask yourself, "What would happen to this situation if I didn't interfere?" If you interfere when you don't need to, you are robbing your child of the chance to experience the natural consequences of his actions. You can also eliminate friction by using natural consequences because you don't have to nag and remind. The situation becomes the dictator. Here are some examples of natural consequences.

Mother recognized that her twelve-year-old Jenny had developed a habit of forgetting things. Luckily, Mother had heard the expression, "A child who always forgets has a parent who always remembers."

One afternoon, Jenny was making a skirt for a home economics class. She was doing the final touches at home and was supposed to take the skirt to school the next morning. However, Jenny was in a hurry leaving for school the following day and forgot to take the skirt with her. Mother noticed that Jenny had forgotten and resisted the temptation to remind her. Instead she was willing to let natural consequences take effect by not intervening.

Later that day, Mother received a phone call from Jenny asking her to bring the skirt to school. Mother told her, in a very friendly voice, "No, Jenny, I'm unwilling to do that," and changed the subject.

Jenny learned to remember from this event. Mother could have nullified the learning experience if she had added a phrase like, "See what happens when you forget?" Then Jenny could have focused on Mother's critical comment rather than on her own responsibility for remembering.

Earlier in this book, it was mentioned that it is the parents' responsibility to filter out those experiences that would overwhelm their child and filter in challenges that their child is able to handle. One mother did an excellent job of combining this with natural consequences. Here's her story:

It was summer vacation and her thirteen-year-old daughter Melissa was going to visit her grandparents for a few weeks. Mother had been concerned about Melissa's irresponsibility in taking care of herself, her clothes, and her money. Since all three responsibilities were going to be important for Melissa to have a successful trip, Mom decided to allow Melissa some learning time.

Melissa needed some new clothes for the trip and Mom asked her how much money she needed to purchase them. Mother had estimated the shopping trip would require eighty-five dollars, but Melissa asked for only fifty dollars. Mom refrained from taking the responsibility to inform Melissa that fifty dollars was not a sufficient amount and instead gave her the money she requested. During their shopping trip, it became apparent to Melissa that fifty dollars was not going to buy many clothes. She voiced this concern to her Mom. Again, Mom stifled her urge to give her daughter more money and lecture her about inability to manage money. When Melissa realized she was going to have to handle the situation, she creatively discovered a solution that amazed her Mother. Melissa accomplished buying a new wardrobe for fifty dollars that included two pairs of shorts, a blouse, and sandals by finding sales and going to discount stores.

On the day of her departure for her grandparents' house, Melissa left her plane ticket on the dresser in her bedroom. Mom happened to see the ticket as she prepared to drive

Melissa to the airport. Mom toyed with the idea of saying nothing (natural consequence), but decided she didn't want to waste a trip to the airport for a missed plane. She felt this consequence would be too severe, so Mom picked up the ticket and handed it to Melissa without saying anything. Melissa sheepishly took the ticket and placed it on the dashboard of the car.

When they were walking into the airport, Mom noticed that Melissa had again forgotten the ticket on the dashboard. At this point, Mom realized they were early and would have time to deal with the consequences of the forgotten ticket, so she said nothing. Halfway to the ticket counter, Melissa gasped, "Oh, my gosh, I forgot my ticket again!" Without words or a look of disgust, Mom handed the car keys to Melissa, who ran back to the car and retrieved her ticket.

Mother allowed Melissa the opportunity to experience the natural consequence of her own behavior. When you allow children these experiences, you discover that the situation can teach lessons more effectively than your words could ever communicate. Another benefit is that when you let the situation do the dictating, your child doesn't try to get even with you by thinking that you were in control and trying to punish him.

What if it is inappropriate to wait for a natural consequence to occur? On such occasions I suggest the use of some steps to resolve conflict. If the misbehavior still persists, then use a LOGICAL consequence.

A logical consequence is a result of the child's action that makes sense to him. Your child must be able to recognize the logic of the discipline in order for it to be effective. For example, if your child broke a window and you took away his TV privileges for a week, the discipline is not logically related to your child's behavior. What has TV got to do with a broken window? Your child is likely to see this as punishment and rebel. On the other hand, it would be logical for a child to do chores (such as mow lawns), to help pay for the broken window. Using this discipline, your child is not being punished, but is learning how to repair his mistakes.

Before I go further into explaining the steps to resolve conflict and logical consequences, there are seven concepts that need to be explained and integrated. They are work on one problem at a time; talk about your problem, not theirs; concentrate on what you can do; set limits to reflect self respect; own your right to your hang-ups; children don't need to suffer to learn; and choose closeness.

1. Work on one problem at a time.

It's important that you work on only one problem until you see improvement. Don't be distracted by other issues because problems are often related. Solving one issue also improves others. If you work on lots of problems at a time, it's easy to become overwhelmed or discouraged.

A Mother was trying to give her attention-seeking six-year old son a choice. "Jim, I want to talk with my friend now, would you either go outside or play quietly in here?" Mom requested. "Guess what, Mom?" was Jim's response. "What?" Mom asked. Without realizing it, she had allowed herself to be distracted by Jim and had forgotten about the choice she had given. Jim continued, "Jerry and I were playing in that old house and we found . . ." Mom interrupted, "I told you not to play there. Don't you know you'll get hurt playing in that old house?"

Mom was no longer working on the first problem of not being able to talk to her friend. She had been drawn into a long discussion about this second problem, playing in an old house. She allowed herself to get distracted from working on only one problem at a time until she was successful. Mother could have given Jim another choice immediately after he did not respond to her first choice, "Would you like to go outside by yourself or would you like me to help you go outside?" Mother could lovingly guide him outside if he didn't respond to this choice.

Do not work on Susie's whining temper tantrums, and not wanting to brush her teeth. Work on one issue until you have success, then work on another issue. You will feel more focused and less overwhelmed when you work on only one issue at a time.

2. Talk about your problem, not the child's!

One of the important steps in creating a logical consequence is to distinguish between what is your child's problem and what is YOUR problem. Often, you are willing to get involved in your child's problems because you have been conditioned to believe that you should be self-sacrificing. How many times have you given your portion of dessert to your child because there wasn't enough for everyone? Or, how many times have you given up what you wanted to do, places to eat, movies to see, etc., because of the kids?

It's only natural that we have a desire to help our children avoid life's pain and suffering. So we push them to take better care of themselves. If we show too much concern for our child's well being, he might misinterpret our concern and develop an attitude of, "It is someone else's job to see that I am happy or to take care of me."

This misconception can be avoided by rephrasing our concerns in a way that demonstrates a model of a person protecting her own rights. To do this we need to talk about our problem and not our child's problem. Instead of saying, "You must learn to pick up after yourself," say "I'm unwilling to allow you to leave a mess in the living room."

On the following page is a list of concerns phrased the way parents often use them. In the adjoining column, the phrases are revised to model self-respect. Consider how you could rephrase other concerns using this model.

As you can see from the Self-Respect Chart, it isn't difficult to revise your concerns into models of self-respect. Your early attempts at using the rephrased statements may be challenging to you, but don't give up. These responses are different from the way your tradition has trained you. In the past, you were programmed to put the desires of others above your own and to feel guilty if you didn't. It will take some reprogramming to stop those feelings of guilt.

An example of owning your own problems follows:

One evening, my husband was sitting in the living room reading. I had gone to bed. After a few minutes, I called out to him, "Honey, you have to get up early in the morning, so you'd better not stay up too long." He responded by saying, "Okay, okay!" and his tone of voice revealed that he didn't appreciate my "nagging." About fifteen minutes later, I asked, "Are you going to read much longer?" He snapped back at me, saying, "I told you, I don't know how long I'm going to read!" At that point, he was determined to read all night!

I changed my approach. Instead of trying to make him feel that I was concerned about him, I talked about my problem. I also gave him a choice. I said, "I have to get up early tomorrow, and when you come to bed late, it wakes me up. Would you be willing to come to bed now and read in bed, or would you be willing to sleep in the guest room when you're finished reading?" My rephrased request evoked a totally different feeling in him; instead of wanting to defiantly read all night, he said, "It's not so important that I read right now. I'll come to bed."

Approaching the discussion by talking about your problem rather than the child's problem is an essential element in resolving the situation. If your approach makes your child feel defensive, it minimizes your chance to win her cooperation.

If you are going to talk about your problem, avoid saying, "Johnny, I have a problem that I want to talk to you about." Even though you are referring to your "problem," the very word "problem" seems to evoke defensiveness. One day, a co-worker said, "Do you have a minute? I have a problem I want to talk to you about." Cautiously following him into his office, I was relieved to discover that the "problem" really was his. From that situation I realized the very word "problem" is anxiety-producing so I suggest that parents say, "I have something I'd like to improve."

You mislead your child when you talk about his problem rather than talking about your problem. When your child sees you spending your energy working on his problems, i.e., "Are you doing your homework?" or "Are you up yet?", then he is led to believe that there is no need for him to be concerned about his personal responsibilities because you are doing them for him.

By rephrasing your concerns so that you own your problems, you will not only influence your child to improve his behavior, also

148

PHRASED AS OVER-CONCERN ABOUT CHILD'S PROBLEM	REPHRASED TO MODEL SELF-RESPECT
"You must brush your teeth or you'll get cavities."	"I'm concerned about having to pay unnecessary dentist bills."
"I don't want you watching TV until all hours of the evening."	"After 9:00 pm, I would like the living room to myself."
"Stop that fighting right now! You'll get hurt."	"I am unwilling to risk breaking my things by allowing you to fight in the house."
"You have to go to school or you won't be able to get a good job."	"When you choose to miss so much school, the teachers call me. I don't know what to tell them."
"Now get a job! You must learn to be more responsible."	"I need your help with the finances and would like you to start buying your own clothes."
"Eat what I have fixed, it's good for you."	"I'm unwilling to prepare different meals for everyone."

he will see you modeling self-respect by changing your <u>own</u> situations, and not interfering in the problems that belong to other people.

Make sure you talk about your problem instead of someone else's. Ask yourself, "What is <u>my</u> problem in this situation?"

3. Concentrate on what you can do.

During conflicts, most of us concentrate on what another person should do instead of concentrating on what we can do. When you catch yourself telling others what they should be doing, stop and ask yourself, "What can I do?"

One evening, during a lecture to about one hundred parents, there were about one hundred noisy kids in the next room. At the start of the program, most of the parents were sitting at the far end of the room from where I would be lecturing. To combat the noise problem, I called to the parents, "Come closer so you can hear better." No one moved, so I said it again, and still no response! I was starting to feel angry at the group and I realized it was similar to how a parent feels when he discovers that he can't control his child. Then I thought, why don't I move over to them? I did, and no longer felt hostile towards them.

I learned two important lessons from this experience. One was that the less we know what to do, the more we know what others should be doing.

The other lesson was that we can use our hostile feelings as indicators of when we are underestimating what we can do. We either don't know what to do or we know what we should do but aren't doing it. So, having hostile feelings usually means that we want someone else to do something to solve the problem.

4. Setting limits reflects self respect.

Parents tend to feel that if they don't talk about their children's problems (i.e., your room is a mess, you haven't taken a bath, etc.) then they will be unable to control their children. The opposite is actually true. By controlling your own actions rather than theirs, you can have a tremendous influence on their behavior without disturbing your relationship with them.

It is crucial to show children that we respect ourselves by setting limits. We can give others as much freedom as possible and we will take whatever action is necessary to establish respect for our boundaries. When a conflict arises, focus on your own behavior-what you are willing or unwilling to do instead of trying to make someone else do something.

A mother and her four-year-old son were walking through a store. The boy said, "Mommy, buy me that toy!" Mom said, "No," and her son started to fuss. Mom's first inclination was to say, "Now, don't ask me to buy you more toys. You know I can't afford it." Instead she just continued walking. The boy took off his coat and threw it onto the floor and screamed, "If you don't buy me that toy, I'm going to leave my coat right here!" Mom stopped and with a smile said, "Tom, I'm unwilling to buy you a toy, and I'm unwilling to buy you a new coat. I'll just wait here until you're ready to go." Tom was shocked but he stood there for a moment and then said, "Okay," and picked up his coat and quietly walked out of the store with Mom.

Here is another example.

One night I was holding hands roller-skating with my daughter. She said in a very demanding tone of voice, "Skate faster!" This wasn't the first time I had noticed that she was being demanding so I said, "I am unwilling to have you talk like that to me. It makes me feel like not cooperating with you and if you continue, I will skate by myself."

I was unwilling to have my daughter talk disrespectfully to me and I told her what action I was going to take if she continued instead of telling her what she had to do.

One couple reported a difficulty they were having trying to get their two boys to lock up their bikes. They complained.

"We've tried everything - punishing them, rewarding them, bribing them, and threatening them. They just keep making excuses and losing locks, chains and keys. We have spent a lot of money on those bikes and we want them to learn to respect their property."

Through the parenting course, the parents began to learn that it's the children's choice to respect their property or not and that the boys were probably feeling resentful when their parents interfered. The parents had to ask themselves, "What is our problem concerning the bikes?"

At a friendly time, the father said to the boys, "There is something I'd like to improve. I've noticed that I've been nagging you guys about locking your bikes. That makes you angry, doesn't it?" The boys looked puzzled and hesitantly answered, "Yeah." The father continued, "I think I've figured out why this bothers me. I realize that they are your bikes and that I gave them to you. It's really none of my business if you choose to risk having them stolen. However, I'll feel bad if the bikes get stolen because they were expensive and I'm not willing to buy you new bikes! Do you guys have any ideas about what I could do to improve on my situation?" The boys answered, "We'll lock them up from now on, Dad."

This was not the first time Dad had heard this promise, so he responded, "Thanks, that will really help. What would you suggest I do in case you forget?" "We don't know," the boys responded. "Well, how about this," suggested Dad. "On the days you choose to leave them unlocked, I'll lock them." "Okay," they responded. "We'll try that for a few weeks and see how it works. If you guys come up with a better idea, let me know, and we'll talk about it," Dad told them.

The very next evening, Dad noticed the bikes were not locked. After dinner, he drove to the hardware store and bought a chain and locked the two bikes to the back porch.

The next morning, Tom, came running in shouting, "Somebody chained my bike to the porch!" Mom resisted the temptation to explain and simply smiled and gave him a pat on the shoulder, then walked away. Five minutes later Tom returned. "I locked my bike with my lock now. Would you take your chain off?" In a friendly tone of voice, Mom replied,

"Dad has got the key and he's at work." Tom asked, "Will you drive us to school." Mom said lovingly, "Sorry, that will make me late to work." Tom and Nate had to walk to school that morning.

When Dad came home and saw the boys had locked up the bikes, he removed his chain. About two weeks later, Dad had to chain the bikes again and from that point on, the boys locked their bikes every night.

5. You have a right to your hang-ups.

When we ask ourselves, "What is my problem?", it might lead us to the conclusion that what we were concerned about is really none of our business. Consider problems such as your son not cleaning his room, or your daughter staying out late. Logically, it is his problem if his room isn't clean and it is her problem if she doesn't get enough sleep. It is their problem. But, being human gives us the privilege of having hang-ups and you do have a right to seek relief from your hang-ups. You have the right to say, "I know that your room is your business, but I have this hang-up. I'm feeling frustrated because having a neat house is important to me and I want your room to be clean. Another way of saying this is, "Even though I have a hang-up about this, I would like you to respect how I feel."

One mother used the above phrase to initiate a discussion with her fourteen-year-old daughter and found it to be the stepping stone to promoting a mutual agreement. The discussion ended with Mother selling the room to her daughter for five cents, so that she would no longer feel responsible. Due to the daughter's pride of ownership and the fact that Mom used an approach that didn't cause the daughter to feel resentful, the problem was solved. Since that time, the daughter has kept her room clean.

If your daughter is not coming home on the agreed upon time and you to say to your daughter, "You must be home by eleven o'clock on weekend nights so you'll get enough sleep," your daughter will probably tune out your communication. Instead say, "I know that you can handle any situation that comes up, but I have this hang-up. When you're out after eleven o'clock, I worry. I don't know if something has happened to you. I'm not sure if I should call the police or wait. Do you have any suggestions as to what I could do about my problem?" If she does not come up with a reasonable response, use a logical consequence which will be explained later in this chapter.

6. Children don't have to suffer to learn.

A word of caution about implementing a logical consequence. It is possible to apply a logical consequence in a way that your child perceives as a punishment, thus making it ineffective. We frequently do this with our choice of words, tone of voice, or by having "that look" on our face. This is difficult to avoid because we have been conditioned to believe that unless a child suffers (i.e. punished), he will not learn. Even though you may consciously deny this statement and say, "I don't believe that," it is still possible that your actions are governed by this subconscious bias. Perhaps this quiz will clarify this point.

A father and his son were in an automobile accident. The father was killed instantly. The boy, who was seriously injured, was rushed to the hospital. A doctor washed up, walked into the operating room, took one look at the boy and said, "I can't operate on this boy. He's my son!"

How do you explain this? If you're thinking things like, the doctor was his step-father or maybe the original father was a priest, then your bias has prevented you from solving this problem. The explanation is that the doctor was the boy's mother. Our cultural bias makes us assume that the doctor was a man. If I had asked you "Do you believe that all doctors are men?" You would probably answer, "Of course not." But it was your subconscious bias and not your common sense that you used at the time when you were confronted with the quiz.

Likewise, at the time when disciplining our children, we often resort to using our bias of "the child must suffer to learn." For example:

A mother who had enrolled her son in summer camp requested that he be assisted in washing his hands before he ate. When he arrived at the camp, I planned a logical consequence for him. At a friendly time, I said to him, "Tom, it's your business if you wash your hands or not, but when you come to the table with dirty hands, you pass germs around. I don't want to get sick. So, unless you have a better idea, from now on I will only serve people who come to the table with clean hands."

That very afternoon Tom put me to the test by coming to the table with dirt on his hands. I calmly reached across the table and removed his plate. Do you know what that kid did? He sat right across from me and smiled through the whole meal while I was boiling inside! He didn't even care that he wasn't eating! Finally, in a gruff voice I said, "You know, you're not getting anything to eat until dinner time!"

I goofed! The consequence had become a punishment. I was now involved in the same power struggle he had with his parents. The thing that got me into trouble was, without being consciously aware of it, I believed that if Tom didn't suffer, he wouldn't learn.

Fortunately, I remembered what Dreikurs frequently said, "It's not so important that you made a mistake. It's what you do afterwards to improve on the situation that counts." Remembering this, I contemplated my mistake and revised my plan for the next dinner.

That evening, as expected, Tom came to the dinner table with mud up to his elbows. Again, I gently removed his plate. Then I said, "Hey Tom, thanks for helping the girls set up their tent. It gave me some time to scout around for firewood." From there, the friendly discussion led to how much fun we all had on the river raft trip the day before.

Later, Tom said, "I'm hungry." I said, "I think we have some extra peanut butter if you want to make yourself a sandwich." He made the sandwich and ate it but he wasn't passing germs around the table, which was my problem. He was happy. I was happy. No one suffered. The amazing part of this story is that the next morning, and from then on, Tom washed his hands before eating. Instead of making Tom suffer, I was firm about not passing germs around the table and I encouraged him and as a result, he learned to do it differently.

It is extremely effective to teach by pointing out what our child has done well. Sometimes this is very difficult to do, especially in the middle of a situation requiring attention and action. We have been convinced that if the child doesn't suffer, he won't learn. In today's democratic atmosphere, the opposite is true. But, as explained in the "doctor quiz," our belief in punishment may exist beyond the reach of our conscious awareness.

A mother and father asked for advice about their three-year-old son messing his pants. They asked, "Should we put him in diapers or training pants?" I answered, "Which would make him feel better?" The parents were shocked by this question, even though they had stated earlier that they did not believe learning required suffering. That question made them realize they hadn't considered that learning could involve something as simple as what made their son feel better.

Frequently, I suggest to parents that they be firm but also arrange it so that their child enjoys the situation. Their response is, "But if he enjoys himself, he'll continue misbehaving!" Invariably, the parents are surprised when they report back the next week saying, "We tried it and it worked!" When your child sees that your intent is not to make them suffer, they become more cooperative.

7. Choose closeness.

In dealing with conflict situations, it's important to shift away from proving who is right and who is wrong. The top priority should be to understand your feelings and the feelings of the other person. All too often in our relationships, we would rather be right than be close. When you acknowledge how the other person is feeling, that person starts to feel understood. As a result of feeling understood, the charge of emotion is dissipated or greatly minimized. Then, and only then, can you come to a resolution that makes you both happy.

When you become involved in a conflict, ask yourself, "Which is more important to me, to be right or to be close?"

STEPS FOR RESOLVING CONFLICT

As often as possible, create win/win situations with your children. The following brainstorming process is the best way I know to create these win/win results. At first, you may find this process cumbersome, but after several applications the process will become efficient and rewarding.

These steps can be used at any time there is a conflict. Later, these steps will be incorporated into a worksheet to design logical consequences.

Problem: three-year-old Joey comes into Mom's bed during the night and Mom is angry that he disturbs her sleep.

STEP 1: Ask the person you are in conflict with for permission to work on a solution. ("Joey, I want some time to brainstorm with you. Is now a good time?")

STEP 2: State your problem as simply and clearly as possible, eliminating guilt, blame, shame and exaggerations. ("It disturbs my sleep when you come into my bed during the night.")

STEP 3: Share how you feel with an "I" statement. ("I feel irritated with you and I don't want to feel that way about you.")

STEP 4: Ask your child to share how he feels and what he wants. It is important to know this in order to find a solution so that you and your child can win. (Joey says, "I get lonely in my bed all by myself. I want to have someone to sleep with.")

STEP 5: Make a list of solutions with your child on a sheet of paper.
   a. Whenever possible, generate ideas where both parties

can win.

b. Let your imagination go wild. Don't limit your ideas to what you think is actually possible.

c. The only rule is that you not criticize or reject any idea until all are on paper and you are ready for Step 6. This is extremely important. If someone becomes negative, the process will not be as creative and it will be less likely that you will find a solution that makes everyone happy. If someone does become negative or critical, lovingly remind him to present a more positive solution. If he continues being negative, stop the process and try again later.

d. Make the process as fun as possible.

e. Encourage each other's suggestions, i.e., "That's a great idea, I never thought of that." or "That gives me another idea!"

f. Be open to new ways of thinking. Don't go into the session with a hidden agenda of wanting it your way. By being open to everyone's solutions, you will be able to generate ideas that are beyond your wildest imagination.

STEP 6: Give the list to your child and have him cross out any ideas that would make him unhappy. It is important that you give your child the list first. Then you cross out any items still on the list you don't agree with. If your child is too young to read the list, read it to him. He can still cross off the ideas he doesn't like.

STEP 7: Pick one of the suggestions or a combination of suggestions that are not crossed out as a solution to the problem.

Suggestions:

a. Make sure both parties are satisfied with the solution.

b. Go for what you want. Don't agree to do anything that you are unhappy about doing or feel resentful about doing.

c. Everyone has veto power.

STEP 8: Use the solution for an agreed upon time period. If the solution doesn't work, start the process over. Learn from failures or mistakes and go forward from that point.

Suggestions:

'THE TWO MULES'
A fable for the Nations

CO-OPERATION
IS BETTER THAN CONFLICT

a. Decide together whether the solution worked.

b. Avoid "I told you so" or blame.

c. Measure successful results based on the positive feelings of those involved in the initial negotiation.

d. Let your failures be your most significant learning experiences and become the building blocks to success.

e. Keep going! Do not quit! Stay positive!

Note: If you are doing this exercise with your family, there is a great game you can play at the same time that will keep the atmosphere fun and encouraging. Get ten colored foam balls, five of one color and five of another color. One color represents the incredi-balls. These balls are thrown at anyone who has an exceptionally good idea as encouragement for his creativity. The other color represents the change-it balls. These balls are thrown at the person who is being discouraging as a fun reminder to keep the process encouraging. This exercise works great at work during staff meetings too.

It is important that when you come to agreement, you are both satisfied with the solution. If you aren't satisfied, one or the other of you will sabotage the process. Sometimes a child says, "sure" to an agreement just to get you off his back and sometimes you are just as eager to get the conflict over with, too. So you settle for a "sure," because it's what you want to hear. If this happens, you can say, "It does not sound like you are happy with this agreement. Let's keep thinking of solutions until we find one that you are really happy with." This process does take time but once your children realize that you are sincere about finding a solution that makes them happy and aren't willing to sell out with a "sure," they'll become more proficient at problem-solving.

At the kid's camp, the kids choose what they will eat for meals. One of the requirements is that they have to promote agreement by arriving at a consensus. The first day of camp it took them over an hour to decide on their first meal. But by the end of the week, they decided on three meals within ten minutes.

Here is the list that Mom and Joey generated:

1. Mom could let Joey sleep in her bed.

2. Joey could stay in his bed.

3. Joey could sleep in Mom's bed twice a week.

4. Joey could sleep in his sleeping bag on the floor next to Mom's bed.

5. Joey could sleep with his stuffed animal.

6. Joey could sleep with his pet cat.

7. Mom could sleep in Joey's bed in his room.

8. Mom could have another baby who could sleep in Joey's room.

Joey crossed out every suggestion except sleep on Mom's bed and sleep in his sleeping bag on the floor next to Mom's bed. Mom crossed out sleeping on Mom's bed when it came to her turn. So the only one that was left was Joey could sleep in his sleeping bag on the floor next to Mom's bed. However, Mom was unwilling to have Joey sleep in her room every night of the week because she wanted some privacy. So they agreed that Joey could sleep in her room two nights of the week. Both Mom and Joey were happy with the solution.

After you have done this process a number of times, you may find it isn't necessary to write all the ideas down. Children are incredibly creative, so don't underestimate them even in the most questionable situations.

If doing the steps for resolving conflicts doesn't work with your child because he didn't follow through with his agreement, then you may need to develop a logical consequence. Using the above example, let's say Joey enters the bedroom with his sleeping bag for the third night. What could Mom do? A logical consequence could be that Mom would take him back to his room and lock her door if necessary.

If logical consequences are to be effective, they must incorporate the following:

THE "4 Rs" OF LOGICAL CONSEQUENCES

1. **Respect** must be shown for your child at all times and he should be allowed to have as much input as possible into the determination of the consequences. Anything that causes your child to feel guilt or shame should be avoided because he will view the consequence as a punishment.

2. The consequences must be **reasonable**. Consequences that are excessive or too harsh will cause your child to focus on what he perceives as punishment instead of repairing the mistake.

3. The consequences should be **related** to your child's mistake. If he makes a mess, he cleans it up. If he hurts someone, he tries to ease the pain. If he damages something, he repairs or replaces it.

4. The goal of the logical consequences should be teaching your child to take **responsibility** for his own actions, not making him "pay" for a mistake.

Special Note: Logical consequences can even be fun and still teach her a valuable lesson.

Remember: Punishment results in your child feeling resentful and angry toward you, but logical consequences teach your child to take responsibility for his own actions.

Logical consequences are set up to improve future behavior, not to punish past behavior. If you are in the middle of a conflict, don't try to develop logical consequences because you'll only come up with logical punishments. Instead, step out of the conflict and take some time to calm down. Then, during a peaceful time, take out the logical consequences worksheet and go through the steps. The following worksheet can assist you in the task of creating logical consequences that will fit the needs of your individual situation.

Notice that this process is the same as the steps to Resolving Conflict except for steps two and seven. The reason step two is so important is because you are probably feeling angry with your child if you tried the steps for resolving conflict and it didn't work. It is extremely difficult to think of fun, creative solutions when you are angry. The purpose of step two (think of three things you love about your child,) is to change your attitude so you will think of a true consequence instead of a punishment.

POSSIBLE RESPONSES

There are several possible responses your child might make when you are developing logical consequences, on page 164 is a list of possible responses and a recommendation on how to handle

LOGICAL CONSEQUENCE WORKSHEET

STEP 1. Write the specific behavior you would like to improve upon with a logical consequence.

STEP 2. List three things you love about your child.
A.
B.
C.

STEP 3. Write what you want to have happen in this situation and why.

STEP 4. Write what your child wants and why.

STEP 5. Generate a list of all possible solutions with your child on a separate sheet of paper.

STEP 6. Create a solution to the problem from the list. Start by having your child cross out suggestions which are unacceptable to him. Then you cross out suggestions that unacceptable to you. Choose one suggestion or a combination of suggestions and write down the solution everyone has agreed upon. It is essential that everyone is happy with the solution or it will not work.

STEP 7. Acknowledge your child for cooperating. Say, "Thanks for working this out with me. What should I do if you happen to forget?" Now generate a logical consequence using either your child's suggestion, which works best, or your suggestion. Once you have discussed and agreed on a logical consequence, write it down.

Logical consequence:

STEP 8. After you have used the logical consequence ask yourself, "Did I get results that were good for my child and me? Do I need to improve the logical consequence?"

them.

Response A:

When asked if he has any ideas about what the consequence could be, he may say, "I don't know," or he may
remain silent. Respond by saying, "Then how about if I try this
. . . If you think of a different plan, let me know and we'll
see what we can work out."

Response B:

He may suggest a workable solution or one that could
work after the two of you agree on slight modifications. If you
agree with his suggestion say, "I'll try that for a week.
Thanks."

Response C:

He may suggest a solution you are unwilling to try.
Respond by asking, "I am unwilling to try that solution. Do
you have any other suggestions?" If no further suggestions are
made, then react as in response "A.".

Response D:

He may suggest a punishment. Example: "If I don't do my
room, you can spank me." Respond by asking, "I'm unwilling
to do things to hurt you because I love you. I already feel
badly and I think it will only make things worse if I spank you.
What else do you suggest?" Don't get fooled into thinking that
if he selects his own punishment, that makes it okay.

Response E:

He may say, "I won't do that anymore." Respond by
asking, "Thanks, that will make things a lot better for me (be
sure you thank him for his promise). What would you like me

to do if you decide to break our agreement?"

If you read the worksheet but didn't take the time to fill it in, telling yourself that you'll go back and do it later, you might want to rethink that decision. Changes rarely occur through reading alone. Taking the time to think it through and write down improves the likelihood of success.

Logical consequences can be done also without using the steps to resolving conflict. Below are two examples.

LOGICAL CONSEQUENCE EXAMPLE

Mom: "Sue, do you have a minute?"

Sue: "Sure, Mom."

Mom: "I have something I'd like to improve on. I've noticed that I've been yelling at you a lot lately and I bet that makes you feel bad."

Sue: "Yeah. "

Mom: "The reason I'm yelling is that on days that you decide not to take out the garbage, I feel like I have to do all the work. What do you think I could do about my situation?"

Sue: "I don't know."

Mom: "Well, how about if I try this. I don't want to be telling you what to do. You can choose to take the garbage out or not. If by four o'clock you haven't taken it out, then I'll do it instead of driving you to soccer practice. In other words, I'm willing to be the chauffeur or the garbage person, but not both. Is that okay with you?"

Sue: "Oh, I'll take the garbage out, Mom."

Mom: "Thanks, that will help a lot. What should I do if some morning you forget? We all forget sometimes."

Sue: "Nothing. "

Mom: "I'm unwilling to do that. How about we try what I've suggested? If you think of a different plan, let me know and we'll see what we can work out."

Another Example

During interviews with an eleven-year-old boy who had been diagnosed as "hyperactive," he constantly fidgeted with things, jumped around, and changed the subject. After a couple of sessions I told him, "Tony, when you fidget with things and jump around, I've noticed that it makes me feel like you're not interested in what I'm saying. Then I start feeling angry with you. I know that you can do several things at once and I know that you really are interested, but I still feel ignored. What do you think I should do when I start to feel this way?" Tony responded, "I don't know."

I asked Tony, "How about when you get involved in something else, I'll stop and wait until you finish?" He said, "Okay." I had to stop about six times in that hour but in the next session, I only stopped three times. After that, he made eye contact, talked, listened, and sat quietly through our hourly sessions.

If you created a logical consequence and discovered that it didn't work and actually escalated the conflict, then perhaps you didn't really use a logical consequence. It's possible that you may have actually implemented camouflaged punishment.

It has been my experience that the most effective consequences are the ones in which the child does not suffer but may actually enjoy the outcome. This is especially true with children who have the goals of revenge or power.

One evening a family with four young children was being interviewed. When the children were out of the room, Mom and Dad complained that they had a lot of trouble getting the kids to help with the household chores. Mom and Dad would ask, remind, plead, threaten and yell. The kids would promise, then forget, ignore, refuse and dispute.

A logical consequence was suggested. The parents were to tell the kids, "We are unwilling to do all the work around the house. From now on we would like you guys (the four children) to take care of clearing the table, putting the dishes in the dishwasher and cleaning the kitchen. We don't want to nag about it because when we nag, we all get mad at each other. However, we are unwilling to cook in a messy kitchen. If by five o'clock the kitchen isn't clean, we will all go out for hamburgers."

The parents and several people in the audience objected. "If you go out to eat, the kids will love it. They'll never clean the kitchen!" We suggested that they try it anyway for one week. It couldn't make things worse because the kids weren't currently doing their chores and the parents had nothing to lose.

Next, I talked to the kids. Their ages were three, six, eight and ten. We told them what their parents were going to do. Their initial reaction was, "Oh boy, hamburgers. We'll never clean the kitchen.... Well ... maybe sometimes.... But if we go out every night Mom and Dad will run out of money. Yeah ... Maybe we can clean the kitchen and then still go out, but only once in a while!"

The audience and the parents were amazed. They had under-estimated the kids. They didn't know that when young people are left with responsibility, they have the ability to be very reasonable. The follow-up report verified that not only had the kitchen chores been done without nagging, but the family was having more fun together as a result.

LOGICAL CONSEQUENCES CAN BE APPLIED

An applied consequence is where you take action that is logically related to your child's behavior. If your child spills his milk, you hand him a dish rag.

Mom was continually nagging her two children to unroll their dirty socks before they put them in the clothes hamper. She decided to try a logical consequence. She simply didn't wash socks that were rolled up. After two weeks, all the rolled up socks were still in the hamper and Mom said nothing. A few days later she noticed that all the socks were still in the hamper, but someone had unrolled them. From that day on, both kids were more diligent about unrolling their socks and a word had never been spoken. The family atmosphere had not been disturbed, the kids didn't feel "bossed" and consequently there was cooperation.

Following is a chart on the distinctions between natural consequences, applied consequences, and logical consequences.

Natural Consequences Involve:

1. A natural flow of events
2. The adult not interfering, arranging or imposing

Applied Consequences Involve:

1. An immediate decision being made and no previous consequence being agreed upon
2. No previous discussion with your child
3. Logically relating the consequences to the behavior
4. A one time procedure.
5. Arrangement by an adult

Logical Consequences Involve:

1. Guidance and arrangement by adult
2. Discussion, understanding, and agreement by your child
3. Relevance to his behavior
4. Being used when a good relationship is in existence

CONSEQUENCES WITH TEENS

When developing logical consequences with teenagers you may want to also consider the following:

1. When you say, "It's your decision," you must mean exactly that. Often we disturb the relationship by getting angry or disappointed that they don't make the choice we wanted, even though we said, "It's your decision."

2. Teens are sensitive to double standards such as, "Dad, if you drink, why can't I?"

3. Teenagers often respond to adult inquiries by saying, "I don't know," or "I don't care." This is usually a way for the teen to get even with the adult. If your teen responds this way, question what you may be doing that he is interpreting as hurtful. Start repairing the relationship by doing enjoyable things together and by encouraging him.

4. We all know that lecturing gets us nowhere, especially with a teenager, yet we keep doing it. "You know when I was your age I not only was going to school, but I also had a full-time job."

You get better results when you draw out their thinking. "You mentioned you wanted more money and I'm unwilling to give you a larger allowance. So how else might you be able to get the money you want?"

Advice given without a request from the teen, often falls on deaf ears. You may want to ask, "Would you like a suggestion?" before you give advice and honor a "no" answer.

You are usually aware when your teen is tuning you out. When you see this happening, stop and ask yourself, "What could I change about my approach? Am I lecturing, trying to control, telling him I know better or being moralistic?" These considerations may help you revise your approach so that you can be more effective.

5. During the teenage years, your child is in the process of emancipation. Peers become as important, or more important, than family. This can feel threatening because we sense we're "losing" our son or daughter. Sometimes when you feel threatened, you may start criticizing their friends but this tactic will only create more distance between you and your teen. Remember, your job as a parent is to gradually work yourself out of a job. Instead of criticizing their need for freedom, acknowledge them for their independence.

6. On occasion, teens may be threatened by your claims that you "understand them." They often don't want to be understood, especially by an adult because they feel that their problems are

unique. They are also threatened by your determination to get them to share their feelings so that you can better understand them. This may be related to their striving for emancipation.

Here is an example of forcing the issue.

"Sara," Mother complained, "how come you never tell me anything anymore? You always used to when you were younger." If you sense a struggle, "I'm not going to let you understand me," you may want to respond by simply accepting their desire for distance and not forcing the issue. Honor their wishes.

Ironically, we sometimes do things to make children mistrust us when they are small (spank, criticize, dominate, etc.) and then we complain that they won't talk to us when they become teenagers. Dreikurs wrote in *Children the Challenge,*

"The tragic, outstanding difficulty between teens and adults is the absence of communication. These doors can be kept open during adolescence. Much of this depends upon our ability to respect our child, even when we disagree with him."

Logical consequences are the replacements for traditional reward and punishment methods. Perhaps someday, three or four generations from now, most parents will just naturally use logical consequences because this process will have been part of the way in which they were raised. Until that day though, it is our task, as the current generation of parents and grandparents, to create logical consequences since most of us didn't experience them in our own childhoods.

*****

RESULTS OF DISCIPLINE

Often we discipline our children in order to get immediate relief from a situation we feel is getting out of control. When our child throws a temper tantrum in the waiting line of the grocery store, we feel embarrassed and try an expedient solution such as threatening or another form of intimidation. The child becomes compliant, but at what expense? When we use this approach to discipline we don't often think of the short term and long term results of our discipline. Use the following list of questions to help you evaluate the results of your discipline.

1. What happens to the child after being disciplined? Is he angry? Do you see signs of passive-aggressive behavior? (Does he take out his anger on younger siblings or pets or "get even" in other ways?) Is he fully participating or is he withdrawn and sullen?

2. What happens to the child's self esteem? Is it lowered? Is it enhanced?

3. Does the child feel empowered to repair the mistake?

4. Does the child become more internally motivated? Does the child become more externally motivated? (Internal motivation leads to responsibility and external motivation creates helplessness, compliance, or resistance.)

5. What happens to your relationship? Is communication improved? As a result of your discipline will he be more or less likely to tell you about his mistakes in the future or will he be too afraid? (His fear will show up by lying about, hiding,or blaming others for his mistakes.) Did you win the battle (get the child to do what you wanted) and lose the war (destroy your delicate relationship)?

6. Does the interaction encourage your child to discuss his wants and feelings or does he become hesitant to express his feelings or opinions?

7. Does the interaction improve his ability to solve conflicts in a way that both people win?

8. Does the child learn about his behavior in a way that provides increased choices or does the child learn that he has no choice at all? (Choices lead to responsibility and develop good problem solving skills.)

RECOMMENDATION:

Fill in the Logical Consequence Worksheet. Practice role-playing the consequence with your partner or a friend. Ask for feedback. Then apply this principle with your child.

Chapter 7

IMPROVING COMMUNICATION SKILLS

HANDLING FEELINGS

Many of us were not allowed to express our feelings as children. We were told things like, "Do you want something to cry about? I'll give you something to cry about!" Expressing vulnerability was judged as being weak. Even the dictionary gives a negative connotation for the word vulnerable: "1.) capable of being wounded; open to attack 2.) sensitive to criticism, temptations, influences etc." Who would want to be vulnerable with a definition like that? We need a new definition that features vulnerability as openness; the ability to honestly express how one feels.

In our society, we have a tendency to criticize or try to stop things that we don't understand. This will show up by making children wrong for the way they feel. "You shouldn't hate your sister." Feelings are not right or wrong. They just are. The less we are in touch with and accepting of our own feelings, the more we try to stop our children from expressing their feelings. Below is a list of "feeling stoppers"-things that we do that can stop the expression of feelings.

Scolding or Reprimanding
Making our child feel guilty
Lecturing
Name calling
Solving their problems

Giving advice
Punishing
Moralizing
Humiliating
Pitying
Making fun
Using sarcasm
Rescuing
Assuming
Denying
Minimizing
Interrupting

If you do any of these when a child is expressing his feelings, you will see that he will automatically stop that feeling in order to protect himself. It is as if he is saying, "It isn't safe for me to express who I really am. I had better stuff this feeling."

Speaking of stuffing, one of the typical ways that we stuff our emotions is by eating. I watched a mother and a little boy who was overweight eating in a restaurant. The mother was incessantly nagging the boy. As she nagged, he stuffed food into his mouth as fast as he could. Another way unexpressed emotions surface is to show up as an illness or the child who feels dominated by his parents and unable to express his feelings may take his frustrations out on his younger siblings, pets or other property.

An emotion repressed, persists. An emotion expressed, dissipates.

The following examples are ways that you can communicate to invite the expression of another's feelings:

- Affirm the feeling: "I can understand why you are angry."
- Listen intently. Pretend your boyfriend/girlfriend were talking to you on your first date.
- Explore with curiosity: "Does your brother do other things that make you mad?"
- Be empathic: "If I were in your shoes, I would probably feel the same way."

- Invite expression of feeling: "How does that make you feel?" or "Tell me more."
- Ask questions to help your child solve the problem: "What would happen if...?"
- Find something about what he is expressing to encourage him: "You're really clear about what you want to have different."
- When appropriate, share a similar experience of your own to help your child feel that he is not alone: "When I was your age, I had trouble asking girls out, too."

When a child expresses emotions, it's important you first acknowledge, affirm or empathize with her before you do any of the other suggestions to invite expression of feelings. The feeling of being understood and accepted is crucial in helping children work through their emotions. If you do one of the other suggestions first, children are more apt to get frustrated or defensive and stop expressing themselves.

Frequently, all we need to do is just listen intently and to hold the child.

One time when I was telling my husband something that discouraged me, he started to give me advice. I could feel myself drifting further and further away and getting more discouraged. Finally, I said, "Would you just hold me right now and tell me that you understand?" He held me for a few minutes and I felt much better. Later, he told me how relieved he felt by giving me comfort and not having to solve my problem.

We get ourselves into a lot of trouble when we feel we have to heal, fix, rescue or convert.

MINIMIZING FEELINGS

One day at lunch, I asked my husband Brian when he was going to visit our daughters. (Brian has three daughters from a previous marriage that live four hours away from us.) He said, "I told them I would come down on Thursday and stay

175

until Saturday." I said, "I would like for you to check with me before you make promises to be gone like that." He said, "Well it isn't written in stone, the plans are flexible." I responded harshly, "Whether it's written in stone or not is not the issue." He said, "That was rather mean (referring to my tone of voice)." I thought about that for a few minutes and responded, "I guess I was feeling that my request was not important," I responded. "You're right," Brian admitted, "I did minimize your request and I will discuss arrangements with you prior to making final plans from now on." I could feel the tension in my body dissipate with Brian's understanding. I felt closer to him because of his empathy.

Notice that when Brian minimized my feelings, I responded in a way that created distance in our relationship. When he acknowledged my feelings and told me what he would be willing to do, he restored the closeness.

Another important point is when Brian described to me what he felt ("That was rather mean.") in a non-judgemental tone of voice, it caused me to reflect on why I said what I did. I was not consciously trying to be hurtful. Because his non-judgemental comment brought it to my awareness, I could then be at choice consciously as to whether I wanted to create closeness or distance in our relationship.

It is really important that you express how you feel instead of harboring grudges. It would have been easy for either Brian or me to be quiet about how we were feeling and continue to stew about how inconsiderate the other person was. But we chose closeness instead.

WHEN SOMEONE SAYS AN UNLOVING COMMENT

While I was writing this book, Brian made a comment that I didn't understand. So I asked him a question about it. He answered angrily and I told him not to get angry. We continued the discussion, but it was very tense and unsatisfying. Later, I found out that when I asked him the question, he thought I was challenging him. I told him that I wasn't challenging him, that I felt he had something important to say and somehow I had missed it. As a result, Brian felt relieved and we were close again.

When he responded unlovingly I could have saved a lot of time and tension by asking him, "What are you feeling?" instead of telling him to not be angry.

COMMUNICATION SKILLS

Let's say that your child takes your jewelry to play with and doesn't put it back. One way to respond would be, "Why do you always take my things? I can never find them. If you don't stop taking my things, I'm going to lock my door!" In this example, Mom over-exaggerates and threatens her child. Most likely her child will get defensive or tune her out. To communicate so that the other person is open to listening, try this model.

> I feel....
> When you....
> Because....
> What I want is....
> What I love about you is....

So, here is what Mom could have said using this model.

"I feel frustrated when you take my jewelry because when I want, it isn't where I left it. What I want is for you to put my jewelry back where you found it. And what I love about you is your sense of style." (If you try this method and it does not work try using a logical consequence.)

WATCH THEIR RESPONSE

In communicating with your children, take responsibility for <u>what you say</u> as well as for <u>what they hear</u>. Watch facial expressions and body posture to make sure your child is not feeling discouraged by your communication. A good clue to a child feeling defensive is when he starts explaining himself, defending himself, rolling his eyes, getting quiet or looking disgusted. If this happens, focus on your relationship first and do some encouraging to create an open atmosphere.

FAMILY MEETINGS

Living closely together is challenging and requires cooperation. I recommend that you have family meetings once a week. These meetings help children feel like they are involved in family decisions and, as a result, they feel more responsible to the family. Family meetings can create an incredible feeling of support and provide a forum for everyone to express their opinions in a safe place. In order to create that safety, it is essential that no criticism be allowed during these meetings.

It is also important that you set a day of the week and a specific time to have your meetings. I would suggest that you make that time a sacred one and that there be no exceptions or changes made to that time. If you keep making changes and exceptions, then your family members may stop respecting the meetings altogether. Below is a list of things your family might consider discussing at the meetings.

- Coordination of everyone's schedule for the week
- Meal planning
- Vacation planning
- Family chores
- Conflicts between family members
- Everyone's goals for the week and how the family can support them to accomplish their goals
- Personal issues for which someone wants help
- Encouragement
- Budgeting
- Announcements
- Family entertainment

During a conflict, words are often used as weapons, so save your talking for the family meeting. This will give everyone a chance to cool off. If the conflict is between the children, postponing resolution until the family meeting prevents them from fighting to get your attention.

"Mom, Bobby took my skate board and won't give it back to me!" "Why don't you put it on the family meeting agenda, Sue?" responds Mom.

Family Meeting Guidelines

Family meetings can be a very successful method of enhancing family cooperation and closeness. Here are some ideas for the format of a family meeting.

1. Hold the meeting once a week at a time when everyone in the family can attend. Keep this time sacred - don't keep changing it at everyone's convenience.

2. Take the phone off the hook so there are no interruptions. This helps your children see how valuable these meetings are to you also.

3. Decisions should be made by family consensus, not majority rules. Consensus means that everyone has to agree. If an agreement cannot be reached after a discussion, table the decision until the next meeting. Go for win/win decisions where everyone agrees and is committed to supporting the decision.

4. Elect a new leader and secretary at each meeting. The leader runs the meeting and calls on members. The leadership should rotate every meeting and other members should be encouraged to support the leader. The secretary's role is to take notes on what was discussed and what decisions were reached. This is important for later in the week when there might be a disagreement about what was decided.

5. Begin the meeting with encouragement for each family member. Use words like, "What I love about you is..." or "I'm grateful to you because...". Teach children to say thank you after they receive a compliment.

6. Consider keeping an "agenda" list on the refrigerator and discuss it during the family meetings. As problems come up during the week, write them down for discussion.

7. Teach your children that if they complain, it's helpful to come up with possible solutions. A person who is not a part of the solution is part of the problem.

8. Include a review of the next week's calendar and plan activities together as a family.

9. For more productive meetings, sit at a cleared table with chairs versus a family sitting room. Do not have a family meeting during mealtime.

10. Always end the meeting by allowing the leader to pick a fun way to close it. Suggestions include choosing a bedtime snack for everyone, a dessert for after the meeting, playing a game, or another activity which allows the family to share a special experience.

11. If your children don't want to attend the meetings, check to see what you are doing or not doing to make them avoid the meeting.

12. Make an agreement with each other that if someone does not attend the meeting, that person will still abide by agreements made at the meeting.

13. Take responsibility to make sure that everyone is feeling good when they leave. In other words, don't let unresolved issues fester.

(These guidelines were adapted by Tim and Anne Jordan from the book *Positive Discipline* by Jane Nelson, Ed. D.)

If the meeting has turned into a gripe session, stop the meeting and do something to help the family feel close again. A great way to accomplish this is to have an encouragement feast. The goal is to have everyone looking forward to the meetings and a gripe session is not the way to encourage repeat performances.

During the course of a family meeting it is often necessary to confront children or ask them questions that may, at first, make them feel defensive. It is essential that before doing this, you establish a trusting atmosphere. Once this friendly atmosphere is achieved, you can risk confrontation. Then, even if the child steps back in caution from your approach, you can still maintain the necessary emotional closeness. However, if you confront when the relationship is disturbed, your child feels backed to the edge of a cliff and if he steps back at that point, you have lost him.

Dad: "Joe, can I talk to you a minute?"

Joe: "What?" (Joe responds in a gruff voice. Caution: the relationship is disturbed - mend it before continuing.)

Dad: "Sounds like you're expecting another lecture. Guess I do lecture you a lot, don't I?"

Joe: "Ah, you aren't so bad."

Dad: "Well . . . sometimes I catch myself treating you like you don't know anything and that's not how I feel."

Joe: "Don't worry about it, Dad. What did you want, anyway?" (Dad has now improved the relationship by talking about some of his own imperfections - it is now safe to confront.)

Dad: "Well, I wanted to see if we could work out a better way of keeping the family room clean. Do you have any ideas?" (If Dad had started out directly with this last question, Joe would have a resisted finding solution.)

With practice, you will find that you are able to read your child's response. You will find this a valuable tool for discussing and resolving relationship difficulties in the family meeting.

FIVE STEPS FOR REDIRECTING MISBEHAVIOR

Many parenting techniques have been reviewed up to this point and now you need a system for consistently applying them. To organize your approach, I suggest you follow these five steps.

1. Establish and maintain a relationship of equality and mutual respect.

2. Gain insight into your child's mistaken goal.

3. Help your child identify his mistaken goal in a NON-ACCUSING way.

4. Arrange or allow a situation that makes your child's goal inappropriate.

5. With encouragement, provide opportunities for your child to:
    a. Be helpful and recognize the value of feeling worthwhile.
    b. Cooperate and recognize how much more can be achieved by working as a team.
    c. Participate and recognize the variety and fun that comes from being involved.
    d. Do what he can to make the situation more enjoyable.
    e. Learn that problems do not need to be "fixed", but only improved.

Here is an example of how I used the five steps of redirecting behavior with Tyler.

Tyler was nine-years-old and for several weeks we had been in a struggle. The battles usually ended with us being angry at each other. Even though we always made up, the tension was mounting in the family.

So here are the steps I followed and what happened at each stage.

1. Establish and maintain a relationship of equality and mutual respect.

One day I was sitting on the step with him. I had my arm around him and it was apparent that we were both feeling discouraged about how our relationship was going. I said, "Tyler, I'm feeling real discouraged about how we are getting along. How about you?" Tyler said, "Me too."

Notice how I maintained a relationship of equality and mutual respect by sharing the responsibility for what was going on in the relationship. I was not just blaming him for the problem.

Getting on your child's eye level and using an accepting tone of voice are other ways to create equality and mutual respect.

2. Gain insight into the child's mistaken goal.

I gained insight to his goal by asking myself how I was feeling. I was feeling angry and challenged at every turn. So I felt his goal was power.

3. Help the child identify his mistaken goal in a *NON-ACCUSING* way.

I asked, "Tyler, it feels like we're getting into a lot of power struggles. What does it feel like to you?" He said, "I don't know. Maybe we have the dis-negotiation flu!" I started to laugh and so did he.

Notice how I was non-accusing by choosing the words, "It feels like..." instead of, "You have been really stubborn lately." Other good non-accusing phrases are, "Could it be that....??" or "I am wondering if....?" It is vital that your intention be one of understanding and curiosity and not to get information to manipulate or control your child.

The purpose of this step is to help your child understand what his goal is, since most children are unaware of what they are doing. This step brings it to his awareness so that he has a choice. When he is doing it unconsciously, he has no choice.

It is so important that you say this in a non-accusing way that if you can't, don't say it. You can skip this step. If you say it in an accusing way, your child will get defensive or quit participating.

4. Arrange or allow for a situation that makes your child's goal inappropriate.

"What do you think we could do about it?" I asked. "We could make a signal - put our hand over our heart and say 'power on'!" suggested Tyler. "That sounds like a great idea,"

I responded.

Shortly after the discussion, I asked Tyler to take a bath and we started getting into a power struggle about whether or not he was going to do it. I remembered the signal and put my hand on my heart and said, "Power on!" Tyler smiled and jumped up and took a bath. I was amazed!

Other things that you can use to make a child's behavior inappropriate are natural and logical consequences, doing the unexpected, giving him more appropriate places to feel powerful or any of the other methods that we have discussed to redirect a child's behavior.

5. With encouragement, provide opportunities for the child to:
   a. Be helpful
   b. Cooperate
   c. Participate
   d. Make the situation more enjoyable
   e. Improve upon problems

After his bath, I went into the bathroom and put toothpaste on my toothbrush and he put toothpaste on his toothbrush. We then made funny faces and noises as we brushed our teeth together. We had fun, felt close and enjoyed our cooperation by finding a creative solution to our power struggle problem.

The following is an example teachers can use for redirecting behavior by using the five steps.

Mary is tapping her pencil and disturbing the class. The teacher asks Mary to stop but the tapping continues.

Teacher: "Mary, why do think you keep tapping?"

Mary: No response. Tapping gets slightly louder.

Teacher: "Would you like to know what I think?"

Mary: "I don't care."

Teacher: "Could it be that you sometimes feel important when you can be the boss and show that no one can make you stop?"

Mary: With a grin, "No."

Teacher: "Class, would you be willing to take some time to allow Mary to be the boss today?"

Class: "Sure."

Teacher: "Mary, how many times would you like to be the boss today?"

Mary: "None!"

Teacher: "I think we should give you some chances in case you change your mind. How about this? You can be the boss fifty times today. If you don't want to use any of the chances, then you don't have to. If you use all fifty and it's not enough, let us know, and we'll give you more."

Mary: "I don't want any times!"

Teacher: "That's okay. Use whatever you want." Later that day Mary starts tapping again.

Teacher: In a friendly voice, "Mary, that's one." Tapping stops but resumes five minutes later.

Teacher: "Mary, two."

Teacher: After Mary has been quiet for fifteen minutes, "Mary, I saw you draw a really neat butterfly on your notebook the other day. I'm writing a paper for some other teachers and I was wondering if you would draw a butterfly for me to put on the cover of my paper?"

Mary's teacher first took time to recognize Mary's goal. She helped Mary recognize her goal in a non-accusing way. She then arranged a situation that made it inappropriate. It was impossible for Mary to be important by being defiant, because it is hard to be defiant when you have permission. It is also important to notice that when the teacher started counting, she used a friendly voice.

This situation reminds me of a joke about a newly married couple riding home from the church in a horse drawn buggy. The horse rears up, and the groom says, "That's ONE!" Later, the horse rears again, and the groom says, "That's TWO!" When the horse rears for the third time, the groom says, "That's THREE!" He pulls out a gun and shoots the horse. In disbelief the bride says, "Henry!" Henry replies, "That's ONE!"

When we suggest counting Mary's fifty chances, but we don't intend you to count as a threat. Your tone of voice must be saying, "Mary, I noticed you are showing your power again, and I thought you might want me to help you recognize that. However, I also want you to know that I like you even though you sometimes want to be the boss." Use an accepting tone and have a warm look in your eyes.

Notice that after the teacher succeeded in making Mary's invitations to power struggles inappropriate, she provided her with an alternative way to become important by asking her to draw a butterfly for her cover. She redirected Mary's behavior toward the goal of helpfulness. Another alternative could be to give the child a position of leadership in an activity.

WHAT HAPPENED TO JUSTIN

At the beginning of Chapter 1 there was a story about ten-year-old Justin, and I promised to give the details of how his behavior was redirected.

Justin's parents enrolled him in our summer camp. Before the camp began, I had a discussion with his parents to get information about what behaviors they were attempting to redirect. In the pre-camp interview with Justin's parents, I discovered that Justin was having a considerable amount of difficulty at school. He didn't have many friends, and the school was concerned about him because he would lose his temper at the slightest provocation and start fighting. He had smashed several waste-paper baskets and broken other things. There were several incidents on the school bus when the driver had to stop the bus to control Justin. At recess Justin would have to be restrained frequently by one of the teachers to prevent him from fighting with the other children.

The parents requested that I work to redirect the following behaviors:

1. Justin losing his temper.
2. Not getting along with other kids.

My first task was to gain insight into the purpose of Justin's behavior. When Justin was born he had an inherited skin disease and his ankles were extremely sensitive. The slightest bump would cause pain. If he was accidentally bumped while playing with other kids, Justin would start screaming in pain and revengefully hit his playmates. His parents would then come running to soothe and comfort Justin's pain. It appeared that Justin misinterpreted these early events. Even though his legs were no longer painful, he still continued his attempts to gain attention by "going off" without sufficient provocation.

One of the methods we used to establish a relationship of equals at the camp was to share many of the responsibilities. We also had the campers participate in developing all the rules.

Justin's misbehavior manifested itself the very first day of camp. When he arrived at our campsite, he went running to a spot under some tall pine trees, and shouted, "I get this spot for my tent!" Some girls approached him and requested that he allow them to use that spot because their tent was larger. Justin's response was, "No! I got here first." So the girls found another location for their tent. As Justin proceeded to put up his tent, he discovered that he could not put some of the stakes in because part of his tent site was solid rock. He then went to the girls and asked them to trade locations but they refused. He came running to us, crying, and said, "The girls took all the good spots for tents, so I can't put my tent up!"

I expected that Justin would be trying to get me to soothe and comfort him by falsely accusing others so I responded in a way that would make his demands inappropriate. In a very friendly voice I said "That's too bad." Nothing more was said.

The next day we were having our council meeting. One of the other kids said, "I have a complaint. Justin keeps blaming me for things when I am not doing anything to him."

I saw this as a good opportunity to help Justin recognize the purpose of his behavior. I asked his permission by saying, "Justin is it all right with you if we explain to the group why they sometimes feel this way about you?" Justin gave his permission. I told the group, "When Justin was younger he had a skin problem on his ankles. If he was playing with someone who just lightly bumped him, he would feel a lot of pain and his Mom and Dad would come to him and help him feel better." I continued to explain to the campers while Justin also listened, "It seems like Justin learned that he can get a lot of attention by losing his temper. Maybe at this camp Justin will decide to stop doing that." Justin did not say anything, but chuckled in recognition.

For the next seven days we continued to make Justin's goal inappropriate and he continued to get angry. At a friendly time when we were all sitting around the campfire, I asked him, "Justin, what should we do when you get angry?" His response was, "I don't know." I said, "How about if we all walk away; then we won't be so likely to get angry at you for yelling. When you're finished shouting, come and get us."

The next afternoon we were all having fun with a water fight. Everyone was splashing everyone else and Justin was also playing. Someone splashed him with water, and he "went off." He threw his canteen into the woods and started to scream that we weren't fair to him. We just silently walked away. We went about fifty yards away and sat on the hillside and waited. About fifteen minutes later, Justin came walking over to us. He said, "You guys better not go into the van." I must confess at that point I became worried. What had he done? Did he tear up the van? Finally I asked him, "Why?" Justin surprised us by saying, "Because I saw a bee in there and I wouldn't want any of you to get stung."

For the first time, Justin was showing some consideration for others! I then asked him, "Is it working out okay for you when we walk away, or are we just making you more angry?" His unexpected response was, "No, keep doing it. It really helps me to control my temper."

The next day we noticed several changes in Justin's goals. He first tried being the "I'm hurt" person. "Ouch! Oh, that hurts! I burned my finger!" When we refused to respond to this behavior, he tried to be the "I'm first" person. "I was the first one here! I was first in line!" Then it was, "My Dad got a new car.... Our house is bigger than your house." Justin was shopping for a new way to find his place. When a child starts shopping, it is a good time to start redirecting him into more useful behaviors because his old way is not working and he is looking for a new way to belong. I decided to make him feel valuable as a new way to belong. I asked, "Hey, Justin, how about helping me move this big pile of tree branches to make this campsite look nicer?" We also played cooperative games that stressed the importance of team work and Justin participated happily.

Evidence of Justin's change showed up on the last day of camp. The night before, he had thrown some dirt in another boy's tent. When the boy awoke, he was very angry and started yelling at Justin. Justin walked away and went into the van. The boy followed, but Justin walked out the back door of the van and sat on a rock. The boy came up to him and shoved him off the rock. Justin jumped up and momentarily expressed his usual attitude of, "I am going to blow," but instantly caught himself. In a very calm voice, he said, "I am not going to get angry at you, Bobby." Bobby sighed and said, "Gee Justin, you sure are doing a good job of not losing your temper." They both laughed. "Would you at least help me clean out my tent?" asked Bobby. "Sure," said Justin. "I'd be glad to. I shouldn't have thrown dirt in it in the first place."

Three months later, I attended a conference at Justin's school. His teachers reported that he had only one flare-up in class, and he quickly calmed down on his own. They said that when he got angry, he would talk about it with the physical education teacher. They were planning to return him to a regular classroom because of his improvement.

Justin's changes were not only the result of applying the redirecting principles at camp but his parents were doing a tremendous job of following through with the principles at home which helped make Justin's changes permanent.

WHAT TO DO IF IT DOESN'T WORK

If you have been trying some of the techniques in this book without achieving much success, you may find this checklist helpful.

___I made sure that I did not make my child suffer.

___My tone of voice was not condescending.

___My child felt loved and accepted by me.

___I agreed with both of the choices I gave my child.

___I encouraged my child to voice his own opinion.

___I respected my child.

___I recognized the purpose for my child's behavior.

___My child did not feel overpowered by me.

___I avoided talking too much.

___The consequence I gave was logical.

___I presented an alternate way for my child to feel special.

RECOMMENDATION

In order to program yourself to use these new methods in the heat of the moment, write out an experience in which you feel you acted ineffectively. Referring to the five steps of redirection, go through how you would have done it differently if it happened again. This exercise will help you to become more instinctive in using these principles to respond to your child.

Chapter 8

IMPROVING MARITAL AND DIVORCE RELATIONSHIPS

EMPOWERING YOUR MARRIAGE

It is important to be loving to your children. But it is also important if you are married, or in a coupled relationship, to provide your children with a model of a couple who is loving. So this next section has some tips on how to improve your relationship with your spouse or partner. Some of these you can also do with other family members.

Getting Together

Dreikurs frequently said, "The less we know what to do, the more we know what the other person should do." With this phrase in mind, let's take a look at the difficulties that sometimes occur when a mother and father are trying to agree on what parenting methods to use. Parents will disagree on discipline for the following reasons:

1. One parent is overly permissive or controlling and the other parent tries to compensate.
2. They are in competition over who is the better parent.
3. One or both of the parents feels it is important to be right. Being "right" is more important than being close.
4. Sometimes one parent feels controlled and dominated by the other. When this happens, their child may be subtly provoked to act out against the more dominant parent.

In the case where one parent is too lenient and the other parent is too harsh, it is necessary that you begin to concentrate on what you can do and become less involved with what the other person is or is not doing.

Sometimes it is easier to know what someone else should or should not do than it is to concentrate on improving ourselves. If you are being effective, your spouse will soon be asking you how you did what you did!

There will always be people in our children's lives who attempt to spoil them. There will always be tyrants who are harsh or try to take advantage of them. Children must learn to deal with all kinds of people and situations. Unless you can guarantee your child that you will always be on hand to keep others from imposing on him, then you are doing your child a disservice by becoming over-concerned with how your mate is dealing with him.

The more energy you put into thinking about what the other person should do, the more likely that you will miss some of your own opportunities. If you see that others are not doing the right thing by your children (unless, of course, they are physically or mentally abusing them), do not get involved in futile attempts to make them change. Instead, look at what you can do to teach your children how to deal with it. You may want to ask questions like, "What do you think you could do differently so Dad wouldn't yell at you?" Conflicts always involve the cooperation of all the persons involved.

Why is it so difficult for us to recognize what we can do? Why do we usually try to influence someone else to take action, rather than taking action ourselves? As children, happiness for most of us depended a great deal upon what the authorities decided. Very few of us were raised in ways that taught us to recognize that our actions could influence other people. Instead, we were trained to feel that we had to gain permission. Or to underestimate what we could do, by becoming over-concerned about what others should do. Start a program of catching yourself when you are feeling that others are not doing what you want them to do. Ask yourself, "What can I do?" In a very short time you will be surprised to see how influential you are by being more in charge of your own life.

Recognize that this concept does not replace getting together and parenting as a team. Showing your children a model of teamwork, agreement and cooperation is one of the most valuable contributions a parent can give to his children. I am suggesting that being over-concerned about the lack of teamwork leads to ineffectiveness.

In certain cases, where disagreement between parents is strong, I would recommend family counseling in order to avoid parenting disagreements from unnecessarily disturbing your marriage and your relationship with your children.

Often, because of their role stereotypes, men feel that it is their responsibility to see that the kids do not defeat their mothers. This leaves men vulnerable to being drawn into the conflict. When there is a conflict in progress between the mother and child, men feel the need to put on their armor and come charging to rescue their mates by slaying the dragon. It is important to resist this urge and allow the two of them to solve their own conflict.

Creating A Loving Model

Some parents put more effort into the relationship with their children than in their marriage relationship. They let their children come first or they let their children come between them. The parent-child relationship needs to be kept in perspective: you have to live with your spouse way beyond the years that you are a parent. Your children will love you after they leave, but you will not be an integral part of their lives anymore. And, if you do a good job of parenting, they will go on to live their own lives independently of you. So don't neglect your spouse when building a relationship with your children, instead inspire your children through your loving relationship with your spouse.

Some couples actually stay in an unhappy marriage for the kids' sake. In the meantime, they create much tension, hostility and discouragement. You are not doing you or your children any favors by staying together. Either get help for your marriage or get out. One of the greatest gifts a parent can give his child is that of a model of two people loving, respecting, playing and cooperating with each other.

Handle Issues

Handle issues as they occur or as soon as you can after they occur. Instead of dealing with issues directly we sometimes:

> Deny them (act or pretend that they didn't happen)
> Ignore it and hope that if you do it'll go away
> Talk yourself out of how you are feeling (I shouldn't feel that way because...)
> Justify or make excuses for the other person's behavior (He only said that because he was drinking)
> Ruminate about the issue (go over and over the event in your mind trying to make sense of it)
> Blame your spouse
> Blame yourself (if I had only done . . . he wouldn't act this way.)
> Get even
> Hide behind righteousness (I'm above having those feelings.)
> Pretend that you don't care
> Withhold your love or your communication

We often choose one of these behaviors rather than dealing with the real issue because we are afraid of creating conflict. We are afraid the other person will get angry or leave us, or reject us. We may even feel that what we say or do will not make a difference anyway. It is amazing the closeness that can be created by resolving the issue instead of "going away" from it.

Take full responsibility for what you have created in the relationship. Remember that your thoughts create your reality. In other words, if you have a belief that men are jerks, that is what you will create in your relationships-a series of men who confirm your belief that men are jerks. This was probably the hardest concept for me to "swallow". It was much easier for me to blame the men in my life, than for me to start taking responsibility for what I was creating or attracting in my life.

If something is not going well in your relationship, ask yourself "What can I do differently?" instead of blaming the other person for the situation. I know of no relationship that was improved by blaming the other person, although it is a very tempting activity! You can spend hours creating brilliant justifications about what a jerk your partner is. Instead of blaming, ask yourself, "What can I learn about myself from this conflict?" You may find out all kinds of revealing things about yourself, like "I didn't stick up for what I wanted." or "I was more interested in being right than I was in being close." Having a spouse is like having a live-in therapist in your house only you do not have to pay the hourly rates!

Creating Closeness During Conflict

Here's a tip for success: when you are having a disagreement with your partner, hold hands. It is difficult to be angry when you're holding each other. If you still find that you're wanting to say mean or angry things, simply withdraw from the conflict. Go somewhere where you can be quiet and take several deep breaths. Then visualize how you want the conflict to end. See the things you want to see, hear the things you want to hear and feel the feelings you want to feel. Discover what your part or responsibility is in the conflict. When you get back with your partner start by admitting your part and then telling your partner what you want.

One day my husband had left his dirty clothes in the middle of the bedroom floor and I had to walk over them. Normally he is an extremely neat person. For some reason, seeing those clothes on the floor really bothered me and I told him that (in a not-so-friendly tone of voice). Things escalated and we started digging up old stuff to add to the argument. I decided to withdraw from the conflict and went to the bathroom and got quiet. I asked, "What is MY part in this conflict?" What I realized was that I was getting ready to do a lecture for a group of 400 people and I was scared. (For some reason, I was having difficulty admitting that I was afraid because that made me feel too vulnerable.) Then I visualized what I was going to say to my husband and the way that I wanted it to turn out. I came out of the bathroom and took my husband's hand. I admitted, "Honey, I realized that I am scared of this talk I have to give and I'm not really concerned about your dirty clothes at all. I'm just really scared. Would you please hold me?" He held me and we felt extremely close.

Seeing your part in a conflict is important. But what do you do when your partner is mad at you? Work to get closer instead of adding fuel to the fire. (The exception to this is someone who is physically violent with you.)

Another time my husband and I had a disagreement and I had gone to our room and was lying on the bed "licking my wounds." Brian laid down beside me and just held me without saying anything. I was still feeling hurt and tried to squirm away but he held me so lovingly and tenderly (but determinedly), that my hostility melted away. Soon, I realized that was the perfect thing for him to do. I had been hurt and just needed affirmation that I was loved.

Another way to handle conflict is to find a way to break up the argument by making the other person laugh.

My husband and I had been to a party and I noticed that he was flirting with another woman. I was jealous, angry, and hurt. We left the party and went to the grocery store. I said some angry things to him and this went on for what seemed like an eternity. Finally, he said, "You are right. I was flirting with that woman. What do I need to do to prove to you that it didn't mean anything? Do I have to take my clothes off right here? Would that prove it to you?" I said emphatically "Yes!" thinking he wouldn't actually do it. He had a suit and tie on. First his tie came off, then his jacket, and then his shirt. When he started to unbuckle his belt, I began to laugh and then he laughed. Here were two grown adults, one naked to the waist, in an aisle of a grocery store between cans of vegetables, standing in the middle of a pile of clothes holding each other and laughing! Later on, we had a discussion about the events leading to the disagreement and made some agreements with each other about how we could avoid the situation in the future.

One of the questions I ask myself every night before I go to sleep is, "Is there any communication that I am withholding from Brian? Is there anything that I'm angry about that I haven't communicated?" And if I think of anything, I handle it before I go to sleep.

Let Go Of Grudges

Holding grudges will only hurt you. You <u>will</u> be hurt by those you love - just like it sometimes rains. Holding back so you don't get hurt again, will work against you. The best thing you can do is to forgive and get on with life.

One couple takes a bath together on Friday night. This is a ritual for them and they do it every Friday no matter what. While they're bathing they clear up any communication that they felt uncomfortable with during the week. They don't get out of the tub until they feel clear and close. Then they drain the tub to symbolize letting go of any grudges.

Make Her Feel Special

Take many opportunities to make your partner feel special. When your partner has been gone several hours, greet her or him at the door with a greeting that communicates, "I am so happy to see you."

One time I came home from working all day and Brian met me at the door with a passionate embrace and took the bags of work out of my hands and carried them up the stairs for me. I felt on top of the world because that small gesture made me feel so incredibly loved and cared for.

Nurture Each Other

Touch, hold and caress each other throughout the day to show how much you care. This makes both of you feel really wanted, loved and nurtured. Just be careful that these caresses don't carry the hidden agenda of leading to sex. Otherwise, your partner will be reluctant with affection if she feels it is only a means to an end.

Support Each Other

Never disagree with the discipline of your children in front of them. If your spouse is disciplining in a way that you disagree with, interrupt her and ask her if you can talk to her in the bedroom. In the bedroom, come to agreement and then have her complete the discipline. It is important that you never sabotage your spouse. If you do, your children will pick up on it and use it against you. It is best if you can be unified in your discipline.

Whenever possible, support your spouse's discipline. For example, your child has asked your husband for something and he has said no. Your child then comes to you to see if he can get you to say yes. Make sure you say something supportive like, "Your father has already said no."

Acknowledge your spouse in front of your family and in front of friends. These acknowledgments can be about things done well or aspects of your partner that you value. This will go a long way in building your relationship with one another.

Find out what your spouse's goals and dreams are and support her to be the best that she can be. Make her being successful just as important as your success. If you really want to stretch yourself, make her success even more important than your own.

Surprise Your Spouse

A wife called her husband and asked him to pick up something at the grocery store. At the grocery store, he received a message from her to pick up something at the drugstore. At the drugstore, he got a message to meet her at room number 416 at the Grand Cypress Hotel. He had unknowingly picked up items that were used for a romantic interlude at the hotel. His wife had arranged for a baby-sitter earlier so they could have a romantic, surprise rendezvous and not worry about parental duties.

Alone Time With Your Spouse

It is important that you make time alone for each other. I recommend having a date with your spouse once a week without children or friends and that you also have a vacation with your spouse alone once a year.

A friend of mine comes home from work, says "Hi!" to the children and then she and her husband spend fifteen minutes alone together. They have made an agreement with their children not to interrupt during those fifteen minutes each night. Then they play with the children after they have had time to connect with each other.

The Need To Feel Valuable

Make sure that your spouse knows how valuable he is to you. Most people like to feel needed or valuable. When spouses don't feel valued or important, it creates an opportunity for mischief to occur in the relationship. This issue was a difficult one for me. I always prided myself on how independent I was and my husband would sometimes complain that he did not feel needed. Now, I ask my husband for his advice about my business. Sometimes I take the advice and sometimes I don't. But I frequently tell him how much I value his opinion.

Know What You Want

Be real clear about what you want and recognize that what you want is important. Sometimes when we don't feel like what we want is important or we don't feel like we deserve it, we become manipulative. This creates distance in all our relationships.

Love Yourself

Ask yourself, "If I was a member of the other sex, would I love me?" If the answer to this question is no, I suggest you start working on changing that. You may want to get some help from a therapist or clergy if you are at a loss in where to begin. Unfortunately, when you don't love yourself, you make demands on your partner to make you feel loved. You will create tests for your spouse to pass to see if he really does love you. Sometimes we go to great extremes to get love, like, getting sick, threatening to leave, and so forth. It isn't your partners job to make you feel loved. It is your job to love yourself. Feeling loved is an inside job.

Live Your Dreams

When you are not living your dreams, you put pressure on your relationship because you become unhappy. Who wants to live with someone who is not happy with himself?

Eliminate Competition

Eliminate competition from your relationship. Become truly happy with each other's successes. Comparison is the root of conflict so be delighted with your differences.

In Stephen Covey's book, *The 7 Habits of Highly Effective People*, he speaks about how important respecting and honoring each other's differences is to creating synergy. "Insecure people think that all reality should be amenable to their paradigms. They have a high need to clone others, to mold them over into their own thinking. They don't realize that the very strength of the relationship is in having another point of view. Sameness is not oneness; uniformity is not unity. Unity, or oneness, is complementariness, not sameness. Sameness is uncreative...and boring. The essence of synergy is to value the differences."

Perfection

No man or woman is perfect, so allow your spouse some imperfections. Quit trying to fix your partner! Trying to fix your partner is a way to keep from working on your own issues.

* * * * *

DIVORCE

Hazards Of Feeling Guilty

Some parents become riddled with guilt about getting a divorce. As a result, they tend to overprotect, be too permissive, avoid disciplining or over-function (super moms and dads) for their child in order to avoid hurting them any further. Or, they attempt to make up for the pain they feel they have imposed on their child because of divorce. Unfortunately, your child often misinterprets these good intentions and becomes overly demanding and irresponsible in return. It is best if you can convince yourself that life will always have it's bumps and scrapes and your child needs to learn how to respond to them in ways that are healthy. Divorce is one of those bumps and your child will handle it.

Fears Of Children

Sometimes children are afraid that since you left your spouse, that you may leave them to. They may over-react to being left at a baby sitter, being late in picking them up or simply being out of the their sight. Again, don't deny their feelings. Acknowledge their fear and then assure them of your presence. Instead of saying, "Don't be silly, I was just a few minutes late." Say, "I can understand you're scared. I will never leave you. I may be gone for a few hours (or a few days if you travel) but I will never leave you." (For further information see the section on Handling Feelings.)

One time, Brian and I were having a disagreement and Tyler got extremely upset. When I asked him what was wrong he said sobbingly, "I don't want a third family that I have to go to!" Had I disciplined him for getting upset I would never have known that he was really afraid of another divorce and was over-reacting as the result of those fears. I assured him, "Tyler, I can understand you are afraid, but your Dad (Tyler calls Brian Dad) and I are not even thinking about divorce. Your Dad and I are disagreeing, and we still love each other even when we disagree. Just because you love someone doesn't mean you don't have disagreements.

Children Want Their Parents Back

Another problem with divorce is that children want their parents back together. They will try the craziest things to get you reunited. Sometimes they will sabotage the new relationship in hopes that if they keep you single, you'll get back together with their other parent. The best way to handle the situation is to first be clear about your intention. The more you hold onto the notion that perhaps you'll get back together and the more you don't get on with your own life, the more your child will continue to be in hope, too.

The second thing to do is to allow your child the right to have these feelings. When your child brings the subject up, don't say, "Your Father and I are not getting back together and that's final. I don't want you to ever bring up this subject again!" Instead be empathic with his fantasy and say, "I can understand that you want us back together. I can see that you think it would make you feel better if we were a family again." And then be clear about your intentions. "Unfortunately, that is not going to happen."

They Have A Right To Be Angry

Out of our own guilt or shame about getting a divorce, we might have a difficult time hearing the effect it is having on the child. Children have a right to be angry. Probably the one thing that a child wants most in his life is to have the two people he loves, live together and love each other. Allow your child to express his anger and avoid feeling guilty or shameful about what you did. Here is an example of a discussion one mother had with her son.

> Son: "Mom, I'm really angry that you and Dad got a divorce!"
>
> Mom: "Yes, I can understand that. What is it about the divorce that makes you the most angry?"

Son: "I don't like living in two houses. I don't know where my home is!"

Mom: "It's confusing to you to have two homes."

Son: "Yeah."

Mom: "What else about the divorce makes you angry?"

Son: "I don't like that we live so far apart. (The families lived in different states.)

Mom: "It would be great if we could jump in the car and see your Dad!"

Son: His anger is dissipating and he is cheering up at Mom's last remark. "Yeah!"

Mom: "Is there anything else you would like to ask me or tell me?"

Son: "Do you still love Daddy?"

Mom: "Yes. There is a part of me that still loves your Daddy very deeply. I respect your Dad a lot but I don't want to be married to him."

Son: Satisfied with her answer, he smiles and kisses Mom goodnight.

Notice how Mom invited her son to talk freely about the divorce. There was no guilt, shame or blame in the conversation. She also made sure that his father was spoken about in an empowering way to benefit both her child and the Father.

Make Peace With The "EX"

The "EX". What a horrible term. That term automatically puts that person in the enemy camp. And when you have an enemy camp, there is an automatic guarantee of war. Why do we create enemy camps with "EXS"? Getting a divorce is sometimes a very drastic and dramatic thing to do. Often innocent people get hurt in the process, like our children. One of the techniques people use to take action in life is to create strong feelings about situations. So, we may create strong feelings about our EX to justify why we took such drastic actions. It is much easier to blame someone else for the relationship ending than it is to dig deep within ourselves and change what we need to change about ourselves that would make the relationship work. Oftentimes too, your new spouse is quick to help you make your EX be the "bad guy" because she doesn't want you to go back to that family.

The hazard of making the EX the "bad guy" is that it tears your child's loyalties. Your child is part of you and part of your EX. If your child hears or senses that you feel his mother is the "bad guy", then he feels you are talking or feeling that way about a part of him. Your child loves you both and by you putting down the EX, you are unconsciously asking your child to make a choice between you and your EX. This is not a fair thing for you to do. Not only is it mentally and physically unhealthy for you to hold grievances, it also wreaks havoc on your child's self-concept.

Remember, behind every grievance, there is the possibility of a miracle if you are willing to look far enough. During my divorce, I wrote a list of all the things that I had learned from my husband. I also wrote a list of all the things I was doing differently as a result of our divorce. I was doing a lot of things that I would have never done if I had stayed married. I was actually able to write my husband a thank-you letter for all the good things he had done and had taught me.

One of the skills I've learned that works really well for me, is when I catch myself dwelling on a grievance, I ask myself, "How is this grievance serving me at this moment?" In other words, for what purpose am I holding onto those thoughts or feelings. One time when I was dwelling on a grievance I had with my Ex, I asked myself that question. What I realized was that I was doubting my attractiveness and by dwelling on a negative aspect of my previous marriage, it kept me safe from having to find another relationship. When I realized it was my self-concept I needed to deal with and not my EX, I was able to correct the problem. Soon I was enjoying the fruits of a wonderful new relationship. Remember: behind every grievance is a miracle.

When dealing with your child about divorce, help him concentrate on the abundance the situation offers instead of the lack. For example instead of thinking, "this poor child is from a broken home," help him realize that now he actually has more, not less. He has two mothers, two fathers, more siblings, more toys, and sometimes eight grandparents! I am not suggesting that you deny that divorce hurts, but I am suggesting that you emphasize the benefits.

Speak highly of your EX to your child. Sometimes parents put down their EX because they're afraid that their child will want to live with the other parent. Or, they want to look better than the other parent. Or, they feel hurt and want to hurt the EX the way they feel hurt. One of the most damaging things you can do, though, is to use your kids to continue the battle with your EX. Trying to manipulate your EX through your children can have life-long repercussions for your child. If you have unfinished business with your EX, get it handled in a different way as soon as possible. Children are not meant to be pawns in unhealthy adult games. If you catch yourself doing any of these things and you are having a hard time changing it, seek the advice of a counselor or therapist.

Some indications to you that you have not made peace with yourself and your EX is that your EX will be uncooperative with you. She may limit your visitations or make visitations uncomfortable in some way for you. Or your support payments will arrive late. The children may also pit the two of you against each other. "When I'm at Mom's house, she lets me have all the candy I want!" or "You're mean! I want to go live with my Mom."

Some signals that you have made peace are that you work out visitations so that both of you win. If there is a problem with a child, you can freely discuss it with each other, offering support and suggestions to one another. Just because you don't agree, doesn't mean you have to do battle with one another. You may even go to your children's events together. In general, you let go of your personal issues and put your child's needs as a priority so that the two of you work in cooperation and have respect for one another. When this happens, you truly become a blended family.

If you do not have a peaceful relationship with your EX and you would like to, you will first have to open yourself to the possibility of it happening. You may be thinking, "There is no way that we would go to an event together! Hell will freeze over before that will happen!" If you're thinking these thoughts, you're right, it probably will never happen. You must be willing or open to it before it will happen.

One thing that may help you do this is to visualize how you want it be. Spend a few minutes every day visualizing in detail how you would most want the relationship to be. See and feel how you want your interactions to be on the phone or in person. Everything that becomes a reality began from an idea from your mind. For example, if you are going to build a house on a piece of land, you don't ruminate about how awful it is that there isn't a house on the property. Instead you start imagining in great detail how you want your house to look and how you want to feel when you are inside that house. It is mind-boggling how much energy we waste ruminating and "awfulizing" about life. Be patient, it may not happen immediately, but keep doing it.

EX Avoiding Visitation

Sometimes divorce is extremely painful for the person who has visitation rights. Every time he picks up the children, he may feel it is an instant reminder of his failure to make a marriage work. So, if you notice that an EX is having difficulty keeping agreements with visitation, understand that this may be what he is feeling and make it as convenient and comfortable as possible for him to pick up his kids. One family arranged pick up of the children at the school because that was the most neutral ground for the mother. Remember to never make him wrong to his kids for being late or forgetting dates. This attitude will only make the situation worse for everyone involved and hurt your child who loves your EX very much.

* * * * *

SINGLE PARENTING

Build A Network

One of the most important aspects of single parenting is to have a network to support you. Parenting is a difficult job with two people involved and single parenting is even more challenging. Make sure you have good day care, reliable friends and trustworthy baby-sitters so that you don't feel so alone and drained.

It is tempting to start relying on one of your children (usually the oldest) for extra responsibilities or to be your confidante or sounding board. Make sure that she is not feeling resentful of the new responsibilities and that she can emotionally handle your sharing of intimate feelings. In the personal growth courses I teach, I frequently hear men complain that when their fathers left, they had to take over "husbandly responsibilities" and they felt forced to grow up too early.

Take Care Of Yourself

Make sure that your own needs are being met. Join a singles group or a singles support group. Don't alienate yourself. If you are secluding yourself to revitalize or recharge your battery, that's great. But if you're feeling lonely, depressed or isolated, it's time to start making a new life for yourself. This is a great opportunity for you to start anew.

Dating

If you've been single for a while and you start dating again, it can be a very trying time for you and your children. You'll want your dates to like your kids, so you might become sensitive to your children's behavior around them. Sometimes you might become uptight at the smallest annoyance which only brings more tension into the situation. If you can relax and not be so desperate for everyone to like each other, things will work out for the best.

Sometimes your child might be appalled at the idea that someone might replace his father or mother. He may be threatened by this new person who is now getting so much of your attention. A child's misbehavior is often a way of telling you something she can't verbalize. Be patient with him and draw out his feelings by providing him with safety and a loving attitude.

During the first year of our marriage, Tyler and Brian had power struggles. Brian and I kept doing all the "right" things to redirect him but they were still occurring. During a family meeting, Tyler admitted that he felt jealous of Brian because Brian got to spend a lot of time with me and even got to sleep with me! So I arranged to make special dates with Tyler without Brian and the power struggles dissipated.

*****

BLENDED FAMILIES

My Stepmom Is An Alien!!

It is normal for a child to dislike his new stepparent. If you are a stepparent and you're feeling judged as not "good enough" by your new stepchildren, give up trying to be. No one will ever be good enough no matter if you had more money, were better looking, or were funnier. No one will ever be good enough unless you are the natural parent, so give it up!! Just be patient and above all, be yourself. Don't overextend yourself at your expense. Don't try to be something you aren't to make the child like you because it won't work! Knowing this can be a Godsend. When your stepchild makes a hurtful remark, you don't have to take it personally. It doesn't mean you have to put up with verbal abuse but it does mean that it has nothing to do with you or your character. Remembering this, it will make it easier not to "plug in" to those hurtful remarks.

Taking Sides

One of the pitfalls of having blended families is that we often play the game of choosing sides. Usually it is the original family members versus the new family members. The following is an example of what happened in our newly blended family.

Brian, Tyler and I went roller-skating and started playing a game called "Crack the Whip." Every time that the whistle blew, your group was supposed to "Crack the Whip." I knew that my son wanted to lead us and I also had a strong suspicion he didn't know how. In his head he knew how to lead, but he didn't have the actual experience. In "Crack the Whip," the leader on the end is supposed to be the pivotal person who stops and swings the others around. Brian and Tyler immediately got into a power struggle over who was going to lead. Being in the middle both literally and figuratively, I was being pulled apart because two people I loved were struggling.

The episode ended in all of us feeling angry and none of us feeling like playing that game ever again! Brian began insinuating that Tyler was willful and wrong and that he was unaware that Tyler wanted to be the leader. I was angry at Brian for not being sensitive to MY son (at that moment he became MY son, not ours, and besides, Brian was just the step-dad). I was being over-protective of my son and took his side against my husband. Then I acted huffy and treated Brian like he had done something "wrong," implying that he was being a "bad" parent.

The next day, I was thinking over the situation and I began to laugh because I realized I had treated Brian exactly the same way he had treated my son. What I received was an incredible gift of knowing that whenever I treat anyone like they are wrong or bad (for whatever reason), I only escalate the existing problem. I felt incredibly justified in treating Brian that way because, after all, he was picking on my child. No matter how justified I felt though, it did not create closeness but only accentuated that aching feeling in the bottom of my stomach.

Step-Sibling Rivalry

The natural child of a parent may feel displaced by the new stepchild or feel threatened by his parent's relationship to his new sibling. One teenager expressed her anger by saying to her new step-brother, "Stop calling him Dad. He's not your Dad. Besides you have your own father in New York. That's your Dad!" Again, it is important not to deny the child's feeling. Remember, feelings are not right or wrong - they just are. Sometimes we are too eager and impatient in

211

expecting the children to like each other. You can't force a relationship on your children. If you do, they'll just become more resistant. Time is often the best healer in these situations. One tip might be to plan an adventure that is out of the ordinary to create some bonding with all the children. An adventure like white water rafting will help them learn to trust and depend on each other and it's great fun!

Chapter 9

SPECIFIC SITUATIONS

ALLOWANCES

I believe that children should be given an age-appropriate amount of money for just being a member of the family. It should be given unconditionally and not tied to whether or not they do their chores, etc. In addition, they should be given opportunities for raising extra money, such as doing chores that are not normally a function of their regular chores. Children should also have chores that they do to contribute to the family for which they don't get paid.

It's vital that you teach your child that there is an abundance of money rather than giving him the feeling of scarcity. You teach him this concept by encouraging him to develop and use his own resources for generating money, not by giving him large sums of money.

Watch the difference these two responses create. Amy asks, "Mom, would you get me a phone for my room?" Mom responds, "Honey, you know we don't have that kind of money right now." Compared to, "Mom, would you get me a phone for my room?" Mom responds, "I'm unwilling to spend my money that way. However, I would be very happy to help you figure out the cost of the phone, installation charges, monthly phone rates, and a way you could create the money."

Notice that the first response is giving the child the belief that money is scarce and that there isn't much she can do about it. Also, you send the message that your child should feel guilty for asking you to spend money on herself. The second response teaches your child that the amount of money she has is dependent on how creative, valuable, and resourceful she makes herself.

Watch the things that you say to yourself and your child that indicate that you are not thinking abundantly, i.e., "That's too expensive, we can't afford that..." Don't limit yourself. The only limits you have are the ones that you put on yourself. You are a creative genius and you are either creating excuses and reasons for your lack or you are creating ideas and plans for your abundance. Which one do you want to spend your valuable time doing?

BEDTIME

Bedtime can be a close encounter of the worst kind or it can be a close encounter of the best time. One of the things that will determine which it will be for you tonight, is whether or not you are in a hurry to "get rid of the kids" so you can finally have some peace and quiet.

Earlier, I wrote on how important it is that you take care of yourself. To reaffirm this idea, when you take care of yourself throughout the day, you won't feel like "getting rid of the kids" at night. No one likes to be "gotten rid of," especially kids. They are extremely sensitive to this intention. The more they feel "gotten rid of," the more difficult they will make bedtime.

Step one for making bedtime easier is to take care of yourself throughout the day. Do a peace check several times throughout the day. If you have a watch with an alarm that beeps on the hour, use it as your signal to make a peace check. A peace check is where you check in with yourself and ask, "Am I feeling peaceful right now?" If your answer is yes, you're in great shape. If your answer is no, do something to make yourself more peaceful. Meditate (this can be done at the office or at home), take a walk, take a hot bath, read something soothing, listen to music, plant some flowers, listen to a self-help tape, pray, communicate any withheld communication with someone you care about, exercise or whatever else makes you feel peaceful. Don't smoke, eat, drink coffee or take drugs or alcohol. These things may temporarily ease your discomfort, but in actuality they will only increase your anxiety.

The second thing to do to make bedtime easier is to develop an order and a routine. You may want to start with bringing to your child's awareness that bedtime will be in fifteen minutes. If you abruptly say, "It is time for bed," you will probably be met with resistance. Giving her a time frame allows her time to complete anything that she is working on or to quickly get one more thing done that she was counting on doing.

Start your quieting or winding down time and then don't engage your children in any wild activities like tickling, chasing, wrestling or anything that will give them a "second wind." Other forms of bedtime rituals may be getting a snack and drink (to avoid the "I'm hungry" or "I'm thirsty" stall technique), taking a bath, brushing teeth, reading two books and saying prayers. Don't let your children bargain for more reading time or this ritual will backfire.

It's helpful to have a special bedtime tradition. For example, the last thing we do while we snuggle in the bed together is to ask each other these three questions.

1. What was the best thing that happened today?
2. What was the worst thing that happened today?
3. What was the silliest thing you did today?

Asking these three questions leaves the child feeling loved and close and it gives us an awareness of what happened with each other during the day so we feel more connected. It also helps us to see if there are issues we need to address at a later time. For example, if your child says the worst part of the day was getting teased, you know your child may need help with this issue later. The last question makes you laugh together and reminds you to be silly and not to take life so seriously. Laughter is wonderful medicine.

Just as an aside, did you know that the average four-year-old laughs an average of four hundred times a day and that the average adult laughs only fifteen times a day? Hmmm.

Another game to play at bedtime is "Remember When?" You can tell "Remember When?" stories that are funny, endearing or that bonded you at that time. One story Tyler likes to tell is, "Remember when you were discouraged Mommy and I made you play 'King On the Mountain' on those big piles of dirt. And you had mud up to your knees and on your face and in your hair?!" When you recall these moments, it creates closeness and appreciation of the family unit. This is also a great exercise to do alone with your spouse to create fun and intimacy.

BEDWETTING

Before you try to use any form of discipline with this situation make sure that you check with a doctor. Many times parents have inadvertently made a physical problem a behavior problem and had adverse effects on the child's self-esteem.

If you know his bedwetting is not a physical problem, teach him how to change his own bed and wash his linens. Do not shame or embarrass your child in any way. Sometimes children wet their beds because they are angry. Check to see if there is a situation occurring in your child's life where he is feeling overpowered.

DAWDLING

If your child is dawdling over a project, ask her how long she would like to complete the project. Then set a timer and challenge her to "beat the clock."

KEEPING THE HOUSE CLEAN

There are many creative ways of keeping your house clean. Here are a few that parents from the Redirecting Children's Behavior course have successfully used.

One family has a box they keep in a closet. Anyone can put anything into the box that is found in the public areas of the house, including mom's and dad's things. In order to get the items out of the box, they had to pay twenty five cents into a jar. (They have teenagers, so twenty five cents is not an inordinate amount to pay.) At the end of the month, they take the money that is collected in the jar and as a family, they decide on a family fun event.

Another family had a list of chores and at the family meetings, they chose who would do each chore. The chores would change every time they had a family meeting.

A method that seemed to work well was to time-limit the house cleaning to the amount of time of the youngest child's attention span, which happened to be eight minutes. At the end of eight minutes, they would all quit and do a cheer to celebrate all that they had accomplished as a team. It's amazing what a team can accomplish in eight minutes. They said that the kids used to groan every time they would hear, "It's time to clean the house!" and now they set the stop watch and jump into action when they hear, "On your mark, get set, go."

TRYING TO GET OUT OF LESSONS

You may want to allow your child to have one personal leave day a month from her lessons. She can use it anytime she wants without any questions asked or without you trying to coax her into going.

Sometimes we want our children to take lessons more than our children want to. Make sure your child really wants those lessons. He might want to play the tuba instead. If your child wants to quit, give him a time frame in which he can quit, i.e. "You can quit after three months."

LYING

When a child lies to you, it is important that you don't try to get him to confess. Demanding a confession can be a way of getting into a power struggle with your child. For example:

Mother knows Robin didn't brush her teeth and she says, "Robin did you brush your teeth?" Robin says, "Yes, I did." Mother then responds by saying, "I know you're lying, Robin. Why do you do that? Now tell the truth."

Instead of demanding a confession, find out the purpose of her lie. Is she lying because she is afraid that if she tells the truth, she will get punished or humiliated? Or is the lie to get attention or to hurt you? In the example above, an alternative response might have been:

"Robin, I see you didn't brush your teeth; please do it now." "I did brush them," Robin says. Then Mother gently guides Robin to the bathroom without talking, gives her the toothbrush and walks away.

Notice how Mother did not make a big issue about Robin's lying. Sometimes parents ask their children questions when they already know the answers. This often sets up children to lie.

QUESTIONS TO ASK ABOUT SCHOOL

Have you ever heard this before. "How was school today?" the parent asks eagerly. "Fine," the child replies, giving as little information as possible. "What did you do today?" the parent presses on hopefully. "Nothin'," comes the reply. "How could you do nothing all day?" the parent retorts in frustration. Sound familiar?

Here are six questions that you can ask about school to create open lines of communication with your child.

1. What were three things that you felt good about today?
2. Who did you help today? How did you help?
3. What did you have difficulty with today? What did you do about it?
4. What did your class need to do to be a better team today?
5. What could the class do to help the teacher?
6. What did you enjoy most about learning today?

REDIRECTING PETS!

One day a neighbor asked us to keep our cat inside for the day because she was caring for a wounded bird in her backyard and she didn't want the bird to become our cat's lunch. My cat wasn't very happy with the situation and stood by the door and cried all morning. My first inclination was to tell him to "shut up" in a very gruff voice or chase him away from the door.

I decided to see if the techniques that work so well with children would also work with cats. I said to the cat, in a calm and friendly voice, "Would you like to stay in this room and be quiet, or shall I carry you into the family room?" Needless to say, the cat just continued to meow. I picked the cat up and gently stroked him as I carried him to the family room. I put him down. He came right back to the front of the house and resumed crying by the door. I picked him up again. Again he returned. This routine went on all morning.

I was beginning to feel frustrated and remembered thinking, "This isn't going to work. He's just a dumb cat. He can't figure out why I keep carrying him to the family room. He's probably enjoying how gently I'm carrying him." I caught myself wanting to give up so I asked myself if I was overestimating the cat's ability to learn. I decided to stick with the training program and after carrying the cat out a few more times, I noticed a change in his response. Instead of coming back to the front door and crying, he started crying at the side door. I removed him again and this time he stood in the center of the room and cried.

It was as if he were experimenting, trying to see if I were removing him because of where he was crying. Two more tries and, guess what? He returned to the front room and lay down by the door, <u>without</u> crying! He was quiet until later that afternoon, when he tried crying again. I immediately took him out to the family room and he returned without any further crying. Ever since that time, one trip to the family room is his signal to stop crying.

STEALING

When a child steals, parents have a difficult time being objective. They become extremely concerned and take their child's stealing personally, as if to say, "If I were a good parent, my child wouldn't steal." What is needed in this situation is for the parent to objectively sit down and think about the purpose for their child's stealing. Is my child feeling incapable of getting things for himself in more appropriate ways? Is he doing it for negative attention? Is it the result of peer pressure? Or, is it for excitement or to hurt others the way he feels hurt? The following is an example:

I worked with a six-year old Vietnamese child who was adopted by an American couple. He had been caught shoplifting several times and when I interviewed him, I discovered a terrifying past. A news correspondent had found him huddled in his hut shortly after he had seen his entire family killed in machine gun fire. Since this was a sad experience for him, his adoptive parents, teachers and social workers had tried to compensate for his loss by feeling sorry for him. He had misinterpreted these well-meaning intentions as, "Life gave me a raw deal and now everyone should make it up to me." He could have looked at this same situation from the perspective, "Wow, these people are helpful to me and are trying to get me started in a new life," but he didn't. Instead he developed an attitude and belief that he was entitled to whatever he wanted whether it was his or not.

When considering the purpose for his stealing, it then made sense why he was doing it. It is always easier to deal with a problem that you can understand, because it becomes less threatening. Here is another example of an eight-year old boy stealing and what his mother did about it:

Tim was caught stealing money from his mother's purse for the second time in two weeks. Mother suspected that the reason he might be stealing was because he and his ten-year-old brother had just recently been given the responsibility to purchase their own lunch tickets for school. Apparently, the boys had either lost their tickets or given them away. Mother was being firm about not letting them charge for more than two tickets at school. When the tickets were missing, she wouldn't give them extra money. So, Tim was in a bind. With her suspicion in mind, Mother approached Tim about the missing money.

"Tim, why did you steal the money out of my purse?" she asked. At first, Tim started crying and became defensive. Mother, recognizing that she might have sounded accusing, wisely rephrased her question. "I'm wondering if there is some reason why you might be taking money? With a little talking, we might be able to resolve the problem, then you wouldn't have to feel like you needed to steal. I have an idea why you might be taking the money. Do you mind if I share it with you?" "Okay," Tim said cautiously. He wasn't sure whether Mother was going to remain cool about this issue or whether she was going to get into her usual mode of reprimanding and punishing.

"My hunch is that you're running out of money for lunch tickets," Mother prodded. "Yes, I am," Tim responded. Are you afraid that if you ask me for more money, I'll get angry?" "Yeah," Tim responded as though he was relieved. "How could we improve on that situation?" Mom asked. "It would help if you gave us separate checks for the school lunch tickets," Tim answered. "I'm willing to give it a try," Mom said. "How do you plan to pay back the $1.75 that you took from my purse?" Tim thought for a minute. "I would like to pay you back twenty-five cents a week until I've paid it off." She agreed to that arrangement.

Mother managed to take a very touchy subject and turn it around so that Tim was responsible for his actions and still felt accepted by her.

Sometimes sibling competition can play a role in the purpose behind stealing.

One single mother had a twelve-year-old daughter named Carmen and a five-year-old son named Shawn. Because the mother worked a lot to make ends meet, Carmen was responsible for watching Shawn. This task contributed to an attitude of dominance over Shawn which set up a competitive situation between the siblings. As a result, Shawn became the incapable "bad" child who learned to steal to get Mom's attention.

Mother was inadvertently doing three things to encourage the competitive roles each child had chosen. First she was giving negative attention to Shawn when Carmen would tell on him. Secondly, she allowed and even encouraged Carmen's tattling on her brother. The third thing she was doing was encouraging Carmen to take care of Shawn by paying her to baby-sit him. This was keeping Shawn in a "one down position." He was feeling, "There's no way I can be as capable as my sister, but I can at least get Mom's attention when I steal." So there was a definite purpose for his stealing.

When Mom recognized his purpose, she decided that one intervention she could make to help minimize the competition was to put the two kids in the same boat.

She told them at a friendly time that she didn't like having to decide who stole the items. She also explained, in a *nonaccusing* way, what she saw happening between them. She told them that from then on, she was no longer willing to play detective and jury. If someone chose to steal, both children would be responsible for paying for the stolen item. She also arranged to pay both Carmen and Shawn for baby-sitting each other, rather than just paying Carmen.

You may be feeling as though it was unfair for this mother to make Carmen pay for something she didn't steal. However, how many more times do you think she told on Shawn? Not many. The discontinuing of tattling resulted in Shawn not getting as much negative attention and any negative attention that he did get, was having to be shared with his older sister.

The stealing was also being minimized because Shawn was now earning his own spending money by sharing the task of sitting with his sister. Mother recognized that Shawn was acting incapable because he was in competition with his sister. Instead of falling for his incompetency as she had earlier, she gradually started giving Shawn more responsibility and provided more opportunities for him to be helpful.

Mother changed her attitude and procedures. As a result, Shawn developed a new confidence in his ability to be helpful. Not only did this help him to stop stealing, but he also started doing better at school once he felt better about himself.

SUGAR

For children who have a reaction to sugar, you can do what our family calls, "sugar for the day". We explained to our son what happens when he eats sugar and won his agreement that he would only eat or drink one thing with sugar a day. He has to have his "sugar for the day" before 6:00 p.m. because he will be up until all hours of the night if he doesn't. He gets to have his "sugar for the day" without us questioning him. Doing this has eliminated many struggles.

THE MORNING RUSH HOUR

Here are some ways to minimize the morning rush hour:

1. Have your child organize his belongings: shoes, homework, lunch money, clothes, in a routine place the night before.

2. Establish a regular bedtime and stick to it!

3. Do not wake your child. Give her an alarm clock so that she can be responsible for getting up.

4. Allow yourself fifteen extra minutes in the morning.

TV

One family got tired of battling over the TV. The parents felt that the children were watching it too much but didn't want to dictate to the children what programs they could watch and when. They wanted their children to develop inner control over this issue so they decided to make up tickets. Together the family decided how much television was appropriate to watch and which programs were acceptable. Each ticket was good for thirty minutes and the total number of tickets was limited. When they wanted to watch a program, they turned in a ticket. In other words, if Mathew used up his tickets within the first few days of the week, he couldn't get more tickets until the following week. In this way, the children still had choices and Mom and Dad didn't become TV dictators.

Allow me to get on my "high horse" for a minute. By the time the average child graduates from high school, he will have seen 18,000 acts of violence on television. How do you think this affects his view of the world? We pay more attention to what we put into our gas tanks than what we put into our child's mind and our own minds. Think about it! We wouldn't even consider putting sugar in our gas tanks but look at what we are willing to put into our minds and the minds of our children.

PREVENTION

Below is a summary of the topics to practice in your daily living that will create fewer discipline problems.

1. Take care of yourself.
2. If you're married, make being close to your spouse a high priority
3. Offer genuine encounter moments several times a day to your children.
4. Allow and invite expression of feelings for both your child and yourself.
5. Whenever possible, make agreements regarding situations ahead of time.
6. Keep your word.
7. Promote order and routine.
8. Be open to learning as much as you can about yourself.
9. Eliminate stress and hurry in your life.
10. Have fun.

OUR RESPONSIBILITY

I am writing this section at the risk of sounding like I am an evangelist. But one of the things I espouse is taking a risk - so here it goes. It is too easy for us to be content with, or self absorbed in, what is going on in OUR home. We often don't realize the impact we all have on each other.

Child abuse creates and perpetuates violence. It has been reported that all serial killers were abused as children. According to the Children's Defense Fund, approximately 2.7 million children were abused or neglected in 1991. In 1992, one out of five children was raised in poverty. You might ask, "What's that got to do with me?" Have you been a victim of or do you know someone who has been the victim of a crime? Someone who has been mugged, robbed, raped or committed suicide? That is what these statistics have to do with you. Child abuse is creating violence in our society. What will these statistical figures be in five years, and what will our society look like in five years? Intervention is the only way to alter the escalating crime rate.

Why are these things happening? My answer to that question is poor parenting skills. And if every parent had the goal of creating a safe, loving and cooperative home environment for his children, then children with high self-esteem would be the norm instead of the exception. **<u>Children with high self-esteem do not commit acts of violence!</u>**

IT IS TIME WE ACT NOW!

So what can YOU do? First of all, make raising your self esteem and the self-esteem of your family a priority in your life. Quit all discipline that is based on fear or guilt. Second, recommend parenting books and classes that espouse non-coercive discipline to family and friends and share with them what you are learning. Third, inspire and invite your schools and day care centers to use these principles with your children while they are in school. Most people do what they do because that is all they know and they are eager to learn other principles that work. So take a risk. Make a change!

Additional Resources

Albert, Linda
Cooperative Discipline (for teachers)

Berman, Claire
Making It As A Step Parent: New Roles-No Rules

Brazelton, T. Berry
Infants and Mothers

Brazelton, T. Berry
Toddlers and Parents

Briggs, Dorothy Corkille
Your Child's Self-Esteem

Canfield, Jack
Self-Esteem and Peak Performance

Cantor, Lee
Homework Without Tears

Clemes, Harris, Ph. D. and Reynold, Bean, Ed. M.
How to Raise Children's Self-Esteem

Dinkmeyer, Don and McKay, Gary
Raising a Responsible Child

Dreikurs, Rudolf
Discipline Without Tears (for teachers)

Dreikurs, Rudolf, Grunwald, Bernice and Pepper, Floy
Maintaining Sanity in the Classroom

Dyer, Wayne W.
What Do You Really Want for Your Children?

Faber, Adele
Siblings Without Rivalry

Faber, Adele and Mazlish, Elaine
How to Talk So Kids Will Listen and Listen So Kids Will Talk

Ginott, Haim G.
Between Parent and Child

Holt, Pat
Choices Are Not Child's Play: Helping Your Kids Make Wise Choices

Janoe, Ed and Hanoe, Barbara
The Tale of the Second Mother

Kvols, Kathryn and Hall, Helen
Parenting Guidelines

Kvols, Kathryn and Riedler, Bill
Understanding Yourself and Others

Leach, Penelope
> *Your Baby and Child: From Birth to Age Five*

Main, Frank
> *Perfect Parenting and Other Myths: New Ways to Encourage*

Marston, Stephanie
> *Magic of Encouragement*

Marston, Stephanie
> *Parenting for High Self-Esteem* (Tape Series)

Nelson, Jane
> *I'm On your Side: Resolving Conflict*

Nelson, Jane
> *Positive Discipline*

Orlick, Terry
> *The Cooperative Sports and Games Book*

Quinn, Phil E.
> *Spare the Rod: Breaking the Cycle of Child-Abuse*

Satir, Virginia
> *Peoplemaking*

Segal, Marilyn, Ph. D. and Adcock, Don, Ph. D.
> *Your Child At Play: Birth to One Year*

Segal, Marilyn, Ph. D. and Adcock, Don, Ph. D.
> *Your Child At Play: One to Two Years*

Segal, Marilyn, Ph. D. and Adcock, Don, Ph. D.
> *Your Child At Play: Two to Three Years*

Solter, Aletha J.
> *Aware Baby: A New Approach to Parenting*

Teyber, Edward, Ph. D.
> *Helping Your Children with Divorce*

Thomas, Marlo
> *Free to Be a Family*

Turk, Blossom
> *Living with Teens and Enjoying Them Too*

Weinhous, Evonn
> *Stop Struggling with Your Child: Quick Tip Parenting*

Book Order Form

Redirecting Children's Behavior
Discipline That Builds Self-Esteem
by Kathryn J. Kvols

$11.95 (US Dollars)
Add $3.75 per copy for shipping and handling.
Write or call for a quantity discount.
Prices are subject to change.

Please send:

_____ copies of *Redirecting Children's Behavior* $11.95 each

_____copies of *Parenting Guidelines Book* $ 6.00 each

_____ copies of *Parenting Guidelines* (audio tape) $10.00 each

_____ copies of *Understanding Yourself and Others* $10.95 each

Name_____Telephone_____

Address_____

City_____State_____Zip__

Total enclosed $_____Check Number_____

Bill my _____ Visa_____ MasterCard

Card Number_____Expires_____

Signature _____

Make checks payable and mail to: International Network for Children and Families
P.0. Box 5759
Gainesville, FL 32605-5759

For additional information, call 1-800-257-9002.

You may also, purchase copies of the book through your local Parenting Instructor.

REDIRECTING CHILDREN'S BEHAVIOR™ COURSE!

If you would like to take this
dynamic parenting program
in your area, please call
1-800-257-9002!

The Redirecting Children's Behavior course (RCB™) is a 15 hour, five session course, based on this book. You and your family will gain the following:

For Your Children
- Enhanced self-esteem
- Creative problem-solving
- Development of responsibility and initiative
- Cooperation in the family

For You as a Parent
- Reduced arguing and scolding
- Feeling more positive about your parenting skills
- Learning new skills on how to win your child's cooperation
- Creating a more peaceful family atmosphere

**If you would like to start
your own business teaching this successful, effective
Redirecting Children's Behavior™ course in your
community,
call 1-800-257-9002**

The **International Network for Children and Families (INCAF)** is a worldwide organization commited to creating new generations of responsible children that have higher self-esteem and better cooperation skills.

INCAF was developed almost twenty years ago after the publication of Redirecting Children's Behavior by Kathryn Kvols. This book, resulting courses and international network have been developed using, in part, the teachings of psychologist Alfred Adler and Dr. Rudolf Dreikurs.

INCAF programs, materials and on-going parenting groups provide adults with effective tools for improving both family and professional relationships. **INCAF** provides a strong support system that can help businesses, schools, organizations and individuals encourage the children of this world. The courses are contagious, fun and effective. The following courses and programs are taught throughout the world by trained INCAF instructors.

Redirecting Children's Behavior™
(RCB)

This is a powerful course that teaches practical parenting skills. Participants learn how to create mutual respect, resolve conflicts and build teamwork in all their relationships.

Family Empowerment Series™
(FES)

Every graduate of INCAF parenting courses is invited to participate in follow-up programs to help them remain focused on applying and enhancing their newly learned skills.

Parenting Instructor Network Training™
(PINT)

Upon the completion of the RCB course, individuals may apply for training as an instructor. This 40 - hour training course will provide potential instructors with the skills and materials to begin teaching the RCB program.

Redirecting for a Cooperative Classroom™
(RCC)

This course is for teachers and includes how to make students responsible for their learning and the success of fellow students. Teachers learn how to build teamwork among students and develop a sense of community and support within the classroom.

Customized Workshops

INCAF offers special workshops on request. Examples of workshops that are offered include: "Building Self-Esteem" and "Conflict Resolution."

**"Children are living messages
we send to a time we will not see."
author unknown**

It is imperative that we commit ourselves
to creating peaceful families
because world peace begins at home.

5